THE
MODERN
JAPANESE
PROSE
POEM

THE MODERN JAPANESE PROSE POEM

AN ANTHOLOGY OF SIX POETS

Miyoshi Tatsuji
Anzai Fuyue
Tamura Ryūichi
Yoshioka Minoru
Tanikawa Shuntarō
Inoue Yasushi

TRANSLATED AND
WITH AN INTRODUCTION BY
DENNIS KEENE

PRINCETON UNIVERSITY PRESS
PRINCETON, NEW JERSEY

Copyright © 1980 by Princeton University Press

Published by Princeton University Press, Princeton, New Jersey
In the United Kingdom: Princeton University Press, Guildford, Surrey

All Rights Reserved

English translation rights arranged through
Japan Uni Agency, Kanda, Tokyo, Japan

Library of Congress Cataloging in Publication Data will be
found on the last printed page of this book

Publication of this book has been aided by a grant from
the Paul Mellon Fund of Princeton University Press

This book has been composed in VIP Century

Clothbound editions of Princeton University Press books
are printed on acid-free paper, and binding materials are
chosen for strength and durability.

Printed in the United States of America by Princeton
University Press, Princeton, New Jersey

Preface

The term "prose poem" is one which can be endlessly argued about. What is being referred to here is the literary genre which came into existence in French literature in the nineteenth century, and which the twentieth-century Japanese poets represented in this book certainly had in mind when writing their own prose poems, or *sanbunshi*. Poems in prose have been written in the English language, but there are hardly enough of any real quality to permit the making of an anthology, whereas the modernist movement in French literature (assuming that to begin with Baudelaire) has produced a number of such writings, and the same can be said of Japanese modernism. Almost any French poet with modernist leanings over the past one hundred years will have written something in this form (although there are exceptions, such as Apollinaire), as will also their Japanese counterparts, although over a shorter period. The fact that this cannot be said of poets writing in the English language seems to indicate, not simply a resistance of the language to that form, but rather how little the literatures in English have been truly affected by modernist poetics.

Given the number of Japanese poets who have written such poems it would have been possible to represent certainly thirty, perhaps as many as fifty, with one or two poems each. This idea was rejected since in translation it is quite impossible to achieve an individual voice for any poet in the two or three pages consequently available to each, and also because there are many poets whose work seemed unresponsive to English translation. I had originally planned to include the work of twelve poets, but dissatisfaction with the translations produced obliged me to reduce the number to six. Of these six the first two represent the "New Prose Poem Movement" of the late 1920's; the next two the postwar modernism of the 1950's; and the final two show aspects of the poetic scene of the present day. Except in the case of the last poet, I have translated poems from one volume only in order to give a fairly complete representation of a writer at a particular stage in his poetic career. In the cases of Tamura and Yoshioka, for example, I have given all the prose poems in one book (in both cases volumes containing prose and free-verse poems). I have done this in the belief that the reader should not be a complete victim of the translator's own taste in these matters.

The exception to this is the case of the final poet given, where I have chosen work from all five of his published books of poetry, since his poetic style shows almost no change throughout his career. In this case the decisive factor was whether the poems would "go" or not, and I rejected some poems which seem to me superior to certain of those translated because I could not manage them so as to produce even that small satisfaction which translation provides. The fact that this poet has been given more space than the others indicates not any value judgement, but rather a feeling that he represents something old, something non-modernist which is not found so readily in modern Japanese writing, and which required space to make clear.

NOTE: Japanese names have been given in the Japanese order with surname first. Long vowels have been marked with a macron, e.g., Tamura Ryūichi, except in the cases of certain place names, such as Tokyo, Kyoto, Osaka, Kyushu etc., which have been assimilated into the English language. In the case of less well-known place names, e.g. Ōtsuka, it has been used.

Contents

PREFACE	v
INTRODUCTION	3
NOTES TO THE INTRODUCTION	55
BIBLIOGRAPHICAL NOTE	57

THE POEMS

Miyoshi Tatsuji	59
Anzai Fuyue	79
Tamura Ryūichi	95
Yoshioka Minoru	107
Tanikawa Shuntarō	125
Inoue Yasushi	141
BIOGRAPHIES	167
ORIGINAL TITLES OF THE TRANSLATED POEMS	182
INDEX	185

THE
MODERN
JAPANESE
PROSE
POEM

Introduction

It is arguable that the poem in prose in some form has a much longer history in Japanese than it has in French, for certainly the prose writings of Sei Shōnagon or of Matsuo Bashō could be thought of as poetic prose and, since they readily break up into short sections, as collections of prose poems as well. There is even a genre called the *Fu*,[1] based upon the Chinese form of the same name (a very free verse form by Chinese standards often found mingled with actual prose). *Fu* is appropriately translated as "prose poem" since in Japanese it is in prose, and tends to be a mixture of pictorial description and quasi-philosophical reflection fairly close to some of those prose poems written in France in the nineteenth century which do not truly belong in the modernist tradition. I have assumed that all these writings are not of the genre I am dealing with here, as also the poetic prose of Flaubert or Joyce is not; and I have done this because the poets in this anthology have, on the whole, made the same assumption.

Modern Japanese poetry has been written very much with the French example in mind. Influence from other Western languages has been only slight by comparison. The main reason for this is no doubt the fact that, as Valéry said, with Baudelaire French poetry became international poetry, as it seems to have remained up to, perhaps even beyond, the surrealist movement. Since poetry in English has also been subjected to this same influence there is little to be surprised at here, although in the Japanese case there has also been a fairly wholesale rejection of the native tradition. It is true that the same might be said of one of the streams of modern American poetry (Whitman-Williams-Olson-Creeley), but the change involved has been of a much less revolutionary kind, and it is at least arguable that this is perhaps not the mainstream of American poetry either.

In order to make sense of modern Japanese poetry (and in particular of the mainly modernist kind with which I am dealing here), one is obliged to look at its sources in the French poetry of the nineteenth century. Looking at these sources means giving examples, and I have provided a generous number in my own translations, not because I feel that superior translations are not available, but from a belief that if the reader sees examples of works he can probably read in the original, he can then gain a fairly good idea of what kind of translation I have made of works he cannot read in the same way. In consequence, as the reader observes what has happened to, say, Rimbaud, his sympathy for the Japanese poets should grow.

The simplest distinction between verse and prose is that prose fills up the page and verse does not, verse providing intervals of emptiness for the eye and silence for the ear. Verse also establishes a regularity of rhythm, depending on the principle of repetition, a characteristic which most distinguishes it from the forward narrative movement of prose. This invites an attention upon what the words are in themselves rather than upon only what they signify in context, providing the particular thickness or depth which characterizes poetic language. The danger with such verse is that the set rhythm may lose its proper incantatory function whereby the words are given life, and degenerate instead into the mechanical stresses of rhetoric. Thus the language becomes frozen, virtually dead in its power to signify, leading to a specialized poetic diction in which the word seems to be more an ͑absence, rather than a plenitude, of meaning. The reaction against the alexandrine which characterized French poetry in the eighteenth century and later was directed against what was seen (perhaps mistakenly) as a situation of this kind, a reaction of an intensity which surely no writer of English has felt against his equivalent form of blank verse. Also, by the eighteenth century, the French language had established a rupture between verse and prose of a kind unknown in English, where the powerful rhythms of the Bible and seventeenth-century prose always allowed a bridge between the two; and the turning away from verse to prose which characterizes so much French writing of this period has no counterpart in English literature. The English Romantic reaction against even the heroic couplet is something quite mild by comparison.

In eighteenth-century France this turning away from verse took the form, for example, of referring to novels as poems in prose (as Boileau did), and of considering the "great poets" of the period as being writers of prose rather than of verse. However, ironically, what most of the "poetic prose" of the time represented was little more than a taking over of some of the duller aspects of the verse tradition, its elevated phraseology, its elegant periphrases, its heavily stressed commonplaces.[2] What the movement did indicate clearly, however, was that a real dissociation between the idea of poetry and the forms of verse was taking place.

Probably what gave the strongest impetus to the movement toward prose was the great vogue for translations of foreign poetry at the time, which were almost invariably made in prose. In the early years of the second half of the century there were translations of the *Eddas*, of Ossian, and of Young, which seemed to give their readers more poetic satisfaction than did the efforts of French versifiers. The fact that Ossian was already in rhythmic prose, and Young in blank verse, would obviously have encouraged the choice of prose, and it does seem to be true that the freer form allowed a more faithful representation of certain technical aspects of the original, such as the rhythm.[3] What is also significant is that the translations tended to be brief and fragmentary rather than extended. It was the short works of Ossian which made the most impact, and each English night of Young became, in Le Tourneur's translation, inevitably it seems, a number of French ones. The gradual tendency of Romantic aesthetic (if considered as something extending from the second half of the eighteenth into the twentieth century) to see the short poem as more essentially poetic than the long was perhaps at work here, and by the 1820's the pronounced taste of French romanticism for foreign literatures showed itself mainly in a considerable number of translations of ballads (Arabian, Spanish, Greek, English, Scots, German), all of which were presented in prose since classical French verse seemed incapable of handling such material.[4] Even nowadays the standard French translation of Shakespeare (like most of the English poets) remains in prose; as does the Japanese, after an attempt in the Meiji period to render him in the older, more poetic literary language. The fact that Shakespeare as a poet has to remain a closed book to readers of French and Japanese does not appear to be simply a question of translation per se (German and Hungarian, I am told, have managed well enough), but more a matter of what these two languages are and what their literary traditions have been.

The upheaval which occurred in Japanese literature with its exposure to Western literatures in the late nineteenth century can be seen as a similar movement away from the classically "poetic" toward the wider possibilities of prose, away from the use of standard poetic diction, rhythmical devices, elegance, toward the world of plain statement. Obviously so large a generalization creates any number of possible objections, but the rejection of the classical literary language for that of the colloquial surely has to be interpreted in such overall terms. In the world of prose writing this movement is fairly easy to discern, although it still does not proceed with quite the relentless logic that a literary historian might wish for, but in poetry what took place is harder to make out since it took so much longer. By the first decade of the twentieth century the colloquial language was established as the language of the novel, but in poetry the first successful poems in that language did not appear until almost the end of the next decade. Even after that the literary language still remained in use in some form until the postwar period. (Here I am not talking about the traditional forms of *waka* and *haiku*, but of *shi* or poems.) One of the truisms about the use of the colloquial language in the novel, for example, is that it permitted a directness of approach more suited to personal, confessional statement than did the ornateness of the previous literary style, thus encouraging the "naturalist" tendency to talk about oneself in the modern Japanese novel. The truism is valid enough, but on looking at some of the prewar poetry one finds what appears to be the reverse of this, for really personal statement seems to require either the vigor of a Chinese style of writing (as in the later works of Hagiwara Sakutarō [1889-1942]), or the more emotive rhythms of the purely literary style, as in the case of Miyoshi Tatsuji (1900-1964), who, after his first volume (some of which is translated here) seems to have written in the literary language whenever he wished to write directly from his own experience. This may demonstrate that the "I" of the poem is more of a literary construct than the "I" of the novel (not to say the "I" of real life, as one can see in the difference between the "I" which appears in Keats's poems and in his letters), or it may indicate the tenacity of the old tradition. However, the way in which this tradition has appeared to Japanese twentieth-century poets provides a problem in itself, since the concept of "poem" as it exists in that tradition is not an easy one to grasp.

Traditionally, Japanese has made clear distinctions between its different literary genres, and even today people who write *haiku*, *waka* or *shi* are called by different names, which must all be rendered in English as the same "poet." When the Japanese require a term which will refer to what we would call "Japanese poetry" they speak of *Nihon Shiika*, the character *shi* ("poem") combining with the character *ka* (or *uta*) which is best translated as "song." *Shi* has traditionally meant poems written in Chinese (by Chinese poets or by the Japanese themselves) and *uta* or *waka* ("Japanese song") is applied to the native product. In addition to this difference of the language in which both types were written, there was also a sense (taken over from the Chinese use of these two characters) that the *shi* was written to be read rather than to be sung, whereas the *ka* or *uta* was to be sung and heard, being musical rather than visual.[5] The fact that these songs were written down and that Chinese poems were read aloud does not affect this essential distinction. Thus, when the Japanese first encountered the poetry of the West they considered it as *shi*, and their first attempts at translation (hymns, extracts from Virgil) were into Chinese. One might therefore conclude that the Japanese literary tradition considered the "poem" as something related to foreign literatures.

One may object to the misleading nature of this statement, and maintain that the idea of "poetry" applies as much to the Japanese song as to the Chinese poem. Even so, it would still remain a fact that Japanese poetry has not shown that concern with form, in the sense of a controlled regularity, which dominates Western and Chinese poetry. Although it has its five-seven syllabic rhythm, making breaks in this brief pattern has always been a possibility, since the pattern is not of a kind to encourage rigorous ideas about it. Thus the idea of verse can hardly be applied to Japanese poetry (whereas it fits Chinese poetry well), and it is less misleading to speak in terms of a rhythm. The very simplicity of this basic rhythm seems to have worked against the idea of the long poem. The fact that long poems of a kind exist in the *Manyōshū* would then be explained by saying that the song still had a public function in the society which produced such poems, and that as society changed the song became more of a private affair, restricting itself to the brevity natural to it. Long works after that period tend to be either sequences of short poems, or to surround the poems by prose, although this "prose" tended to be as musical as the "songs" themselves.

The foregoing summary is not meant to be a correct account of the Japanese poetic tradition in its entirety, nor does it represent my own views on the matter. There has been enough research done in this century to show that a stereotyped image of all Japanese poetry (brief and songlike) is inadequate as a description of a more complex reality. What I am attempting to outline are some of the causes of the dissatisfaction many Japanese writers in this century have felt with their own poetic tradition. In the same way, my remarks about the state of French verse as it was seen by writers of the eighteenth century, who turned to prose, are an attempt to account for that movement. As a view of the poetry of the previous century alone (Racine, La Fontaine) they would be misleading, since they do not describe the verse tradition in French, but only a dissatisfaction with it at a particular time. One may see this dissatisfaction as misplaced but still as important, even decisive. This same judgment should be extended to the account of the Japanese situation, since, without it, the whole modernist attempt in Japanese poetry, of which the prose poem in the sense I have defined it here is the supreme example, becomes virtually impossible to understand.

One can grasp the nature of this discontent by considering this image (obviously simplified and only partly true) of the state of Japanese poetry at the time it came into contact with the West. Imagine an English poetry at the time of Browning, which consisted of Medieval lyrics still written in Middle English (but with a vocabulary limited to words of Anglo-Saxon origin), and showing little variation in poetic theme from what had been written centuries before. There would also have been briefer versions of these lyrics, sometimes on more realistic themes than the lyric normally permitted, and they might at times be combined in sequences. The most serious poetry would have been in Latin, which showed little change from the Medieval Latin lyric as it had been written on the continent. One then has to imagine this poetic tradition confronted by the existence of the highly developed literatures of Europe. Clearly, people who saw their native tradition in similar terms (and a number of Japanese people certainly did so) would have felt it inadequate for their idea of what poetry should be. They would have seen this inadequacy as something principally brought about by the traditional form of the literary language, the desire for change being most consciously directed at that language itself.

Even given this discontent, however, the first attempts to put Western poetry into Japanese were in the old literary language, since the colloquial seemed to be incapable of poetic expression. The *Shintaishishō* (*Selection of New-style Poems*, 1882, which consisted mainly of translations, but which included a few original poems) showed an eagerness to expand the vocabulary and themes of poetry. However, the language remained literary with the traditional rhythms, even though it seemed resistant to the kind of subject matter these editors, and later poets, wished to treat. Even as late as 1905 the very influential volume of translations by Ueda Bin (1874-1916), *Kaichō-on* (*The Sound of the Tide*) of mainly French symbolist and parnassian poets, was still in the literary language, and made use of new combinations of what remained the traditional rhythmic patterns. The success of the translations seemed to confirm the viability of a lyrical poetry in the literary language which would lay its main emphasis upon musical values, and this in fact is what the "symbolist movement" in Japanese poetry became. However, the two important poets of this movement, Kitahara Hakushū (1885-1942) and Kambara Ariake (1876-1952), did not write new-style poems for long. Kambara retired from the world of poetry in 1908, and Kitahara, after his volume *Omoide* (*Remembrance*) in 1911, wrote mostly children's verses and *tanka* ("short songs"). One sees the same process of giving up the poem (in this case for the naturalist novel) in a slightly earlier writer, Shimazaki Tōson (1872-1943). These poets created a lyrical tradition which extended in some form up to the Pacific War, which produced perhaps the only twentieth-century poetry to have been read with real affection by the common Japanese reader. But no amount of experimentation with fives and sevens could stand up to the flood of European modernism which entered the country in the 1920's, and the literary language itself gradually became something quite remote from everyday life.

The kind of apathy a Japanese poet could feel toward this poetic tradition can be seen in the case of Nishiwaki Junzaburō (b. 1894). In an introduction to a selection of his works he has given an account of his spiritual development.[6] He writes that his interests at school had been more in the direction of painting than literature, but that there had been young men with a taste for literature, which was much like their tastes for talk about sex, for drink, and for visiting the ladies of the town. He found the way of thinking that all this implied offensive in its vulgar sentimentality, which showed also in the form their interest in poetry took, for they produced *waka* and indulged in *haiku*. Although he amused himself with these people, his true emotional interests were elsewhere. The only poetry he encountered at school which genuinely moved him was Chinese poetry, which he felt to be superb and which made him realize that the poem could be a literary form of great beauty. His own decision to write poetry in English was, as he saw it, the same kind of practice as that of priests and scholars in the Tokugawa period who wrote poems in Chinese. He did not attempt to write poetry in Japanese because that implied using the old-style language, with its outmoded elegance; writing in English meant that he could bypass that problem. Hagiwara Sakutarō's poetry showed him that poetry could be written in Japanese, not only because it used the colloquial language, but also because its "naturalism" was opposed to that romantic sentimentality which, in his view, had infected Japanese poetry, that sentimentality which had embarrassed him so much at school. Nishiwaki's tastes in foreign poetry when young had been for Baudelaire, Rimbaud and Mallarmé, but the writer who had most powerfully affected him was Flaubert, and he had wished to write poems in his style.

This is an account, admittedly edited but still almost word-for-word, of the views of one of modern Japan's most distinguished poets. Since it is a personal statement of why he found the traditional literary language and its implications irrelevant to his own poetic needs, the reader should not be misled into believing this to be any objective account of that language or tradition. One could perhaps take exception to every value judgment made, and Nishiwaki's approval of Hagiwara's naturalism may seem surprising in view of the fact that Hagiwara, on many occasions, expressed his own dislike for that literary movement. But Nishiwaki is referring to something certainly present in Hagiwara's poetry even if the label chosen for it is perhaps confusing.

Hagiwara's dislike was for the *Minshūha*, the "Democratic school" of poetry which came into existence in the middle years of the second decade of the century (at a time when naturalism in the novel had come to an end), and which continued into the 1920s, where it linked up with the proletarian literary movement. Hagiwara's objections, like those of other poets, were that the attempt of the democratic poets to free the poem from the restrictions of the past and create a "free poem" (*vers libre*) had resulted only in a vulgarization of the form into a prolix and characterless prose. He felt that poetry since the *Selection of New-style Poems* of 1882 had been mere exoticism, created out of vague Western influences, and that real poetry could be written only out of genuine, lived experience. This is what Nishiwaki refers to as naturalism; he shared the same belief that what Japanese new-style poetry had so far been had meant the creating of a false, since linguistically outdated, persona for the poet in his poem.

Hagiwara's *Tsuki ni hoeru* (*Barking at the Moon*) in 1917 showed that poems could be written in both free verse and the colloquial language. The poems also have colloquial rhythms often of great subtlety, even beauty. However, the poetic attempt the book represents looks more now like the ending of a tradition rather than the beginning of a new one (the considered opinion of Miyoshi Tatsuji), a tradition running through Kambara and Kitahara to end with Hagiwara. Thus *Barking at the Moon* marks a border-line between old and new, a signpost pointing in a number of directions. The work may have established the colloquial language as one for poetry (with many backslidings, including Hagiwara's own), but what form this was to take remained, perhaps still remains, open. When French modernism was introduced in the 1920s, one of these possible forms seemed to be that of the prose poem.

Japanese poetic modernism could be thought of as little more than a number of responses to waves of foreign fashion (futurism, cubism, dadaism, surrealism), for the leading modernist poetry magazine of the time (*Shi to Shiron*, [*Poetry and Poetics*], 1928-1931) devoted much of its space to the translation of the relevant (mostly French) literature. One can have doubts about the value of the work produced, since nearly all Japanese critics express such doubts, which can hardly be ignored even if the overall judgment they imply need not be accepted. Even so, Japanese poetry has been created out of this modernism, no matter how much postwar poets may say they have rejected it. It is no more possible to ignore modernism in any account of twentieth-century Japanese poetry than it is in the case of the French. If one sets aside various mock-dadaist absurdities (those wilder aspects of modernism which literary history tends to overemphasize) then the making of the prose poem seems to have been the supreme modernist act for the Japanese poet. (This is clear in the case of the two postwar poets translated here, Tamura and Yoshioka, whose prose poems are the most modernist, and most difficult, of all their works.) The prose poem, by definition, denies the rhythmical values which have dominated the lyrical tradition, and sets its emphasis instead upon visual or ideological ones. Thus it is an attempt to get as far away from the tradition of the *uta*, or song, as possible.

Kitagawa Fuyuhiko (b. 1900), a central figure, along with Anzai Fuyue and Miyoshi Tatsuji, in the "New Prose Poem Movement," said in an article in *Poetry and Poetics* in 1929[7] that the new prose poem was written in reaction against naturalist description, and also against the idea of the poet's singing spontaneously. Today's poets were no longer recorders of the inner movements of the soul, nor were they concerned with exposing their emotions. They were technicians who selected from innumerable words those which could be built into one single and perfected construction. The words and phrases were to be fitted together like bricks and, although the cement used should hold, the pattern in which they were arranged was to imply the possibility of other patterns, the perfect construct being an expression of the arbitrary nature of the material arranged.

This statement is an epitome of the anti-naturalist, anti-romantic assumptions of the modernist poet, the central belief being that the poem is an essentially gratuitous construct, autonomous and independent of reality, with the poet as a conscious technician who proceeds with his creation very much as a scientific worker engages in research. This image of the poet has never become strong in the English literary tradition (hardly at all in the British, and not decisively in the American), but it still dominates European poetry, as it also does that of Japan. It is one of the failings of Anglo-American accounts of twentieth-century literature that they still do not fully accept the seriousness and validity of this image. Even if fifty years have seen modifications in modernist poetics, their basic nature remains unaltered, so that a poet of Philip Larkin's kind is, for good or ill, as unthinkable in Japanese now as he would be in French or German. Any understanding of modern Japanese poetry needs some sympathetic grasp of this image, not a parochial dismissal out of hand. Its sources lie in the nineteenth century, along with the masterpieces of the French prose poem, at which I now wish to look in some detail.

The first French prose poems are those of Aloysius Bertrand (1807-1841), posthumously published in 1842 under the title *Gaspard de la Nuit*. Bertrand had clearly tried to write "poems" in prose rather than a merely rhythmic prose, for he rejected the idea of spontaneous lyricism for that of formal precision. His work shows a continual desire to tighten up the poem and so to avoid the tendency of earlier poetic prose toward moralizing meditation interspersed with occasional lyric flights.[8] Bertrand's poems make use of repetitive images, as well as sometimes of repeated rhymes, and have no obviously "poetic" phraseology. His creation of a ballad form based, it seems, upon prose translations of English and Scots ballads, demonstrates how much the question of form concerned him. This in itself points to the basic paradox of the prose poem, since it aims at formal freedom and yet is obliged to realize that, as a poem, its existence depends upon its language being structured. When poets begin to feel that the principal aim of their art is a restructuring of personal experience and thus of reality itself (as Rimbaud believed), then the prose poem is the poem *par excellence*, a true image of that striving toward new structure which the poetic act, indeed the poetic apprehension of the world, becomes. One stage in this process can be seen in the case of Charles Baudelaire (1821-1867), who devoted the last years of his life to such poems.

The prose poems collected after his death as the *Petits*

Poèmes en prose (or *Le Spleen de Paris*) in 1869 are extremely varied, and also uneven in quality. Some of them are merely passages of reflective writing, often of a didactic kind; and there are also those which appear to be simply outbursts of temper. However, Baudelaire has recorded (in a letter to his mother) how much spiritual effort the writing of these poems cost him. It is arguable that the concentration these "*petites babioles*" required may have hastened the end of his sanity, and of his life. In his *Intimate Journals* he has written how there are certain states of the soul in which even the most ordinary of objects reveal the depth of life since they have taken on symbolic status. Traditional verse seemed to transform the expression of such insights into calm, order, and harmony, and Baudelaire may have sensed that prose would give him a greater freedom to reproduce his real vision of the city.

How much he achieved this in his prose poems is debatable, and there is still no consensus about their value. The creative power seems to have left Baudelaire in his final years, and no doubt the last of his prose poems employ an excess of rhetorical devices, of cadenced, formal symmetry, as an attempt to sustain failing imaginative resources. However, those of his prose poems which succeed probably represent the true beginnings of modernism in French literature, and they need to be looked at. The first poem in the volume (but not the first in order of composition) is this: *L'Étranger*.

THE STRANGER

"Whom do you love best, enigmatic man, tell me;
your father, your mother, your sister or your brother?"
"I have no father, mother, sister, brother."
"Your friends?"
"You make use of a word whose meaning to this day remains unknown to me."

"Your country?"
"I know not in what latitude it is."
"Beauty?"
"She I would love most willingly, as goddess, as immortal."
"Gold?"
"I hate it just as much as you hate God."
"Well, what do you love then, you extraordinary stranger?"
"I love the clouds . . . the passing clouds . . . those yonder, over there . . . marvelous clouds."

The poem does not seem to be aiming at statements rationally or meditatively arrived at by any narrative process. The conversation provides a series of negatives, of vacancies, and then the final image of the clouds creates the symbol of an emptiness, which transcends all others to achieve the moment of insight, when the everyday, the commonplace seems to mean something; the Joycean epiphany. Whether the poem actually achieves that or not is a matter for debate perhaps, but clearly it does aim at a poetic statement by way of a pattern which no merely 'poetic' or 'rhythmical' prose would attempt. Whether good or bad, it is a poem.

The next one aims at more than this, and also shows the meditative, forward-moving aspects of ordinary prose, although striving to achieve something beyond that: *Le Confiteor de l'Artiste*.

THE ARTIST'S CONFITEOR

How moving are the ends of autumn days! Moving the heart to sadness, for there are certain sweet sensations whose vaguenesses do not exclude eternity. No sharper edge than that belonging to infinity.

What great delight to drown one's eyes in the enormousness of sky and sea. Solitude, silence, and the incomparable chasteness of their blue. One small sail shudders on the horizon, in smallness and in isolation like my own irremediable existence. Monotonous melody of the swaying sea, and then of all those things of which I think, or through which I think (for in the greatness of the dream the self loses itself); and though I speak of thought I mean it as a flow, or as pictorially.

And yet these very thoughts, either which come from me or come from out of things, these soon take on too much intensity. My over tautened nerves can only give off peevish, dolorous vibrations.

And now the sky's profundity dismays me. The inevitability of the sea, the whole unchanging nature of the sight, revolts me. . . . Ah, must one suffer, or eternally flee from beauty? Leave me, Nature, pitiless enchantress, my always victorious rival. Cease tempting me in my desire and pride. The quest for beauty is a duel wherein the artist screams aloud in fear, before being defeated.

The rhythm of the French is a very musical one, for in his prose poems that striking use of the broken phrase (*phrase heurtée*), the phrase which clashes with its context, which one finds in his journals, almost never occurs, the movement being wave-like, limpid. It is true that Baudelaire's ideas about musicality in language were concerned more with the succession of images, with the pattern of the emotion being drawn true, than with pure sound effects. However, it is questionable how relevant such ideas are to his prose poems, since what one does in fact find is a constant attempt to compensate for the prosiness of prose, by a heightening of the rhythmical and sound effects. In making these translations (both the French and Japanese) I have noticed a tendency in myself to become obsessed with rhythmical rather than semantic questions. The continual reflective effort to stop being so has made this much more a labor than the translating of verse would be. This rhythmic obsession seems to be something which will tend to happen with the prose poem, since the rhythm has to be striven for; a tendency accentuated when put into the heavily stressed English language. There has been a temptation, not always successfully resisted, to drop into a jog-trot blank verse reminiscent of ancient editorials in the London *Times*.

The next poem, *Un Hémisphère dans une Chevelure*, is one of those which have a verse equivalent, *La Chevelure*, and the interested reader might well compare the two.[9] It is the one in prose which seems to come off best, presumably because it is considerably less "poetic" than the one in verse.

A HEMISPHERE IN YOUR HAIR

Let me breathe in long, long and deep, the odor of your hair; let me plunge my face therein, a man quenching his thirst in fresh spring water, swaying it all within my hands, sweet scented handkerchief I wave to shake my memories in the air.

If you could understand all that I see there; all that I taste, breathe in; all that I hear in your sweet hair. My soul is borne away upon this perfume, as other men voyage far on music.

Your hair contains a total dream of the world, of sails, of masts; great seas where the trade winds bear me away to countries of delight, to pleasant climates where the sky is bluer and more deep; the air is perfumed with the scent of fruit, of leaves, of human skin.

There in the ocean of your hair I glimpse a harbor filled with mournful chants, thronged with the vigorous men of every nation, with ships whose complex, delicate superstructures stand out against a sky, in whose immensity the eternal heat reclines.

In the caressing of your hair I find once more the languorous indolence of those long hours spent upon my couch, there in the cabin of some elegant ship, surrounded by potted plants and stimulants, swung by the unfelt sway of the harbor water.

Before the glowing fire of your hair, it is a mingled scent I breathe; tobacco, opium, sugar. In your hair's night I drown intoxicate, confused in odors of ship's tar, of coconut oil, and of musk.

So let me bite, long, long and deep, upon the black, the heavy tresses of your hair. With your rebellious and flexile hair within my mouth, I seem to feed upon my memories there.

This poem (like the following one, and also somewhat like the preceding one), employs brief, balancing paragraphs quite similar to those of Bertrand. In fact the more successful of Baudelaire's prose poems do tend to employ this almost verse-like form, which suggests that the devices of balance and repetition were something both he and Bertrand required if they were to write a "poem." When Baudelaire did not make use of such techniques his prose poems became something with the virtues of prose, but none of the energy of poetry, nor its peculiar organization of meaning. In this next case, *Chacun sa Chimère*, and in the poem above, the use of prose has perhaps allowed some form of escape from the various restrictive dignities imposed by a constant verse rhythm; but one also feels that this might have been more happily achieved through a freer verse form, and did not really require anything as drastic as prose. Since this next poem is indeed one of his finest in this form, it arouses doubts about the whole enterprise as such.

EACH MAN HIS OWN CHIMERA

Under a great, grey sky, in a vast, dusty plain, with no roads and no grass, no thistles and no nettles, I came across several men with bent backs walking.

Each one bore on his back a huge chimera, as heavy as a sack of flour or coal, or the equipment of a Roman soldier.

And yet each monstrous beast was no dead weight. In fact quite otherwise, for it held and squeezed its bearer with its rippling, powerful muscles, firmly clinging onto its mount by digging two great claws into his breast; its fabulous head surmounting that of its man, like one of those horrible helmets whereby ancient warriors had hoped to inspire more terror in their enemies.

I talked to one of these men, and asked him where they went. He said he did not know, nor did the others; but that obviously they must be going somewhere since an irresistible urge to walk impelled them onward.

One curious thing to note: none of these travelers showed any sign of annoyance at the beast clinging around his neck and to his back; so it would seem they did in fact consider them some actual portion of themselves.

Nor did their serious and exhausted faces give any witness either to despair. Under the splenetic vaulting of the sky, plunging their feet into an earth as desolated as the sky itself, they moved on forward with the resigned expressions of people condemned always to have hope.

So this procession passed me by, and went off into the haze of the horizon, that place where the round surface of the planet removes itself from human curiosity.

Then for some moments afterward I tried to understand this mystery. But irresistible indifference soon clamped down on me, and I was more heavily weighted even than they, each under his chimera's crushing burden.

In this poem that tendency in Baudelaire for the attempted symbol to fail to work symbolically and take on mere allegorical meaning (to such an extent that some question just how much he can be called a "symbolist poet"[10]) seems to have been avoided; a refutation, indeed, of the doubt just voiced. It also achieves a complexity of tone which often the restrictions of verse seem not have allowed him; this can be seen even more clearly in the final example, *À Une Heure du Matin*. It has two verse equivalents, *L'Examen de Minuit* and *La Fin de la Journée*,[11] the second of which is also given here in translation.

ONE O'CLOCK IN THE MORNING

Alone at last! You now hear nothing but the rumbling by of one or two belated, worn-out cabs. For a few hours we shall have some silence, if not rest. At last the tyranny of the human face has disappeared, and I shall only be inflicted with myself.

Now at last I am allowed to soak in a warm bath of darkness. So double-lock the door; an act which will augment my solitude, and strenghten those real barricades which separate me from the world.

Foul life in a disgusting town! So let's go back over our day again. Saw some literary men, one of whom asked me if you could travel overland to Russia (he assumed, no doubt, that Russia was an island). Then had a good row with the editor of a review, whose sole reply to my objections was that "we are on the side of decent people here," implying that all other journals were being brought out by a load of crooks. I then paid my addresses to twenty people, fifteen of whom were quite unknown to me, shaking a corresponding number of their hands without, unfortunately, having taken the precaution of buying gloves beforehand. During a shower, so as to kill time, I ascended to the room of a dancing girl, who begged me to design her outfit for the role of Venus. Then called on the director of a theater, who suggested, as he showed me to the door, that I "should be very well-advised to see a certain Mr X—the most thick-headed, foolish and most celebrated of all my writers—no doubt you could really make it if you worked with him. We'll see how it turns out."

Then I boasted (I don't know why) of certain bits of villainy I'd never in fact done, and also cowardly denied performance of some other misdemeanors committed with some pleasure at the time; the sin of wanting to show off, a crime against all human decency. I then refused a friend something which would have been no trouble to me, and wrote a recommendation for a total idiot. Ugh, is that the lot?

Sick and tired of all, especially of myself, how I would wish now to redeem myself, regain my self respect a little, in the silence and the solitude of night. Souls of those I have loved, souls of those I have sung, strengthen me, sustain me; remove me from the lying, the corrupting mists that hold this world. And Thou, O Lord my God, give me the grace to create such poems as will prove to me that I am not the lowest of all men, that I am not inferior to those whom I despise.

THE END OF DAY

It runs, in the wan light,
Twists and dances endlessly,
Clamoring shameless life.
And so when finally

On the horizon night arises
Voluptuously to appease

> For all, even hunger, and effaces
> All, even shame, the poet says:
>
> "Now soul and backbone ardently
> Require rest; with heart
> Thoughtful of mortality
>
> I wish to lay me down, apart,
> Covered with your curtains, night
> Shadows which will refresh me."

It is dangerous to make literary judgments from translations, but the following statements could, I think, just as reasonably be arrived at from a reading of the originals. There can be little doubt that the prose poem is more moving than the one in verse; that it achieves a much more varied tone, and that the distance between the poet and the reader seems much less than in the piece of verse. The wonderfully achieved movement in the prose from the protective ironies, the mingled self-hatred and self-love of the earlier lines, to the impressively passionate and dignified outburst at the end, allows the writer to express *himself* in a way which the verse does not achieve, perhaps does not really permit even. For example, the poetic persona in the verse poem attempts to be complex and ironical; not a straightforward lyrical posture but a self-critical, self-amused one, as can be seen in this third stanza:

> Mon esprit, comme mes vertèbres,
> Invoque ardemment le repos;
> Le coeur plein de songes funèbres,

Here the rhyme of "vertèbres" and "funèbres" is of a comic kind reminiscent of some of Byron's; but instead of acting in such a way as to seem to reveal the poet to the reader, it has the contrary effect of making him seem more affected, more distant, as if he were merely playing at self-irony in order to hide himself behind a more complex mask. Similar devices in the prose poem really do seem to bring the poet closer to us, although I have no wish to make any claim about the goodness or badness of this, but simply to indicate the profundity of the differences between the two ways of writing. It may well be, in fact, that what the prose poem most indicates is a distaste for the kind of artifact the poem has always been, for the distant perfection, the apartness from the world which belongs to all traditional art. Thus the prose poem aims at something other while still being obliged to attempt to create new perfections of its own, since art unavoidably aims at such. This restlessness, this refusal to establish a fixed form, this always striving for the new, is the essential nature of modernism—a modernism which achieves its finest expression in the nineteenth century in the prose poems of Arthur Rimbaud (1854-1891).

The title of Rimbaud's volume of prose poems, *Les Illuminations*, refers not only to the spiritual state of being "illuminated," but also to the "painted plates," the English subtitle of the work. This pictorial concern of the nineteenth-century prose poem is something which needs to be stressed. Bertrand's *Gaspard de la Nuit* was a quite deliberate attempt to create paintings in words, and Baudelaire's own profound interest in painting makes it reasonable to assume that the basic impulse behind the making of *Le Spleen de Paris* was the wish to be the kind of "painter of modern life" he so admired in Constantin Guys.[12] It is the motionless quality of these images which is so like that of the painting; surprising in prose which does not naturally achieve any kind of static moment as the painting does, but continually moves forward. What makes many of the French nineteenth-century prose poems reminiscent of the cinema is that, when they are obliged to show some process of change, as prose, perhaps as even language itself must oblige them to, then they do this by a "cutting" from one image to another which is not (at least in prose terms) obviously related to it. This is true to a considerable extent of Baudelaire (of all the poems given here except perhaps the last one, although even in that case it is true to some degree despite the fact that it observes the normal movement of prose more than the others). It is also undoubtedly the most striking feature of Rimbaud's *Les Illuminations*, as one can see in the following example, *Enfance*, a poem in five sections of which I give the second and third only.

CHILDHOOD
II

She is there, the little dead girl, behind the roses — the young mother who died comes down the steps — the cousin's carriage screeches on the sand — the little brother (he is now in India), before the setting sun, there in the meadow full of pinks — the old ones whom they buried upright in the wallflowered rampart.

Swarms of gold leaves surround the general's house. They are in the South — You follow the red road till you come to the empty inn. The great house is for sale; its shutters have come loose — the priest will have taken away the key of the church — around the park the keepers' cottages have no one in them. The fences are so high you only see the tops of trees. There's nothing to see inside there anyway.

Meadows rise up to hamlets with no weathercocks nor anvils. The floodgate is raised up. Oh the Calvaries and windmills of the desert, the islands and the stacks of hay.

Magic flowers hummed. The banks held him and lulled. Animals of a fabulous elegance wandered there. Clouds were gathering over a high sea, made of an eternity of bitter tears.

III

In the wood there is a bird. His song arrests you and you blush.

There is a clock which does not strike.

There is a muddy hollow and a nest of white things in it.

There is a cathedral which descends; a lake which rises.

There is a small cart now abandoned in the brushwood, or which comes running down the path with ribbons flying.

There is a troupe of costumed players, seen on the road through the borders of the wood.

And last of all, when you are hungry, thirsty, there is someone who chases you away.

Here the prose poem has ceased to have much to do with what is traditionally thought of as prose, the continual tendency being to liberate the phrase, or the word itself, from the restrictions of any syntactical context. Rimbaud's well-known criticism of Baudelaire for the old-fashioned nature of his poetic forms could be applied to some extent to Rimbaud's own early verse, much of which is either derivative or else rejection, in the form of obscene parodies, of those who had previously been his masters. He seems to have turned to prose as a way of not writing verse, rather than from any desire to employ prose devices for poetic purposes. Prose offered Rimbaud language in its naked form, something freed from its literary and social traditions. In the example given above this produces a truly remarkable achievement, for I know of no other short piece of writing which conveys with such completeness and power that great emptiness which the child's perception of the world tends to be. The form of the poem seems to give the actual pattern of so many inner experiences of that age which it is usually impossible to name, yet alone describe. This has been achieved because, indeed, the poem has almost no concern with any "descriptive" act in the normal, traditional meaning of that word. There is no sense of connections being made, but only of the act of naming itself.

Les Illuminations are not all of this kind (indeed, the constant variety of the prose poem is something already referred to), and there are examples where the traditional flow of prose is made use of, although not for traditional purposes, as in this next example, *Ville*.

TOWN

I am an ephemeral and not too discontented dweller in a city thought of as modern because all known taste has been excluded from the furnishings and the exteriors of its houses, as well as from the design of the town itself. Here you will discern no trace of ancient superstition. Indeed, morality and language have been reduced to their simplest forms of expression. These millions of people who have no need to know each other manage their education, work, and their old age, in so very similar a fashion that the extent of their lives must be several times less long than some foolish statistic has worked out for the peoples on the continent. Consequently I see from my window new spectral shapes wandering through the thick, eternal smoke — our woodland shade, our summer night — new forms of Furies, there before my little home which is my fatherland and where the heart is since every place around here is exactly like it — and then Death without tears, your energetic girl and handmaid, Love in despair, and a pretty little Crime whimpering in the muddy streets.

In this case the use made of prose seems to be to indicate that the language of the editorial, in which the work starts, is no description of our nightmare but only an actual part of it, for eventually it has to speak of things about which its rational premises do not properly allow it to speak. The sense of break in the poem at the point, "Consequently I see . . . " ("*Aussi comme* . . . ") is not truly connected with any alteration in the movement of the prose, but in the logic of the things being talked about; as if prose were being stood on its head at that point.

One can see a similar process being performed, this time with the prose of lyrical regret, in the next example, *Ouvriers*.

WORKERS

Ah that warm February morning. An untimely southern wind had stirred the memories of us foolish paupers, our young poverty.

Henrika had on a cotton skirt of white and brown check, something which must have been worn in the previous century, a ribboned bonnet and a silk scarf. It was much gloomier than if she had been dressed in mourning. We were taking a turn around our suburb. The weather was overcast, and this south wind had raised up all the vile smells in the ravaged gardens and the wasted fields.

It cannot have tired her out as much as me. In a strip of water left by last month's downpour on a fairly high-up path, she pointed out to me some tiny fish.

The town, its smoke and noises of its trades, followed us for a long way down the roads. You other world, some habitation blessed by sky, by shadows! The wind from the south recalled to me the wretched happenings of my childhood, summer despairs, the appalling quantity of power and knowledge which fate has always kept so far from me. No, we shall not spend summer in this mean country, where we will never be anything but plighted orphans. I wish that this arm of mine grown hard no longer drag with it a *darling image*.

The lovely, rhythmical prose invites a sympathetic, almost a sentimental reading of this; which is then upset by the final line which calls for a second reading of a much harsher kind, leading to that bitter undertaste which marks his writing when it appears to be letting itself go in a way traditionally thought of as "moving." The poems in which such ambiguity does not exist are only those which aim at presenting experiences which have not yet been described, and so are not yet corrupted, since they are beyond normal language, as in *Aube*.

DAWN

I embraced the summer dawn.

Still nothing yet stirred on the front walls of the palaces. Dead water still. The camps of shadows had not yet left the road on through the wood. I walked, awakening breathings loud and warm, and the precious stones looked on, and the wings rose noiselessly.

My first venture, on a path already full with fresh pale bursts of light, was a flower which told me its name.

I laughed at the blond *wasserfall* with tangled hair among the pines: on the silvered peak I recognized the goddess.

And so I lifted one by one her veils. In the avenue by waving of my arms. On the plain where I told the cockerel all about her. Through the great town she fled among the domes and steeples, and running like a beggar over marble quays, I chased after her.

High on the road, near to a laurel wood, I wound about her all her layers of veils, feeling a little her enormous body. Dawn and the child fell deep down in the wood.

When I awoke it was midday.

One could hardly have a better example of modernism's desire to remake the world, to restructure actual experience in language that has been made new. The same is true of the next poem, but in this case one's doubts as to its success lead to a further doubt concerning the whole modernist undertaking. *Barbare*.

BARBARIC

Long after the days and the seasons, after the beings and the countries.

The flag of meat bleeding on the silk of seas and arctic flowers (they do not exist).

Regained from old heroic fanfares—which still attack us in the heart and head—far from the old assassins.

—Oh the flag of meat bleeding on the silk of seas and arctic flowers (they do not exist).

Sweetnesses!

Braziers, raining in squalls of frost—Sweetnesses! —fires in the rain of the wind of diamonds by the terrestrial heat eternally turning to carbon for us—Ah world!—(far from old refuges, from old flames, which one hears, one feels).

Braziers and froth. Music, turning aside of gulfs and crash of icicles on the stars.

Ah sweetnesses, ah world, ah music. And these shapes, sweat, hair, eyes, all floating. And white tears boiling—ah sweetnesses—and the female voice which reaches to the depths of volcanoes, the arctic caves.

The flag....

This poem satisfies all the demands of modernist poetics; the word freed from the tyranny of syntax, the symbol freed from the allegorical requirements of precise signification, the apprehension of the world freed from traditional rationalizations, and language given so much freedom of association that any part of it can signify a whole universe. Yet one result of this is a set of limitations as severe as any of those imposed by the past, for a concern with the as yet unnamed, or with the unnameable, suggests that only experiences of an imprecise, and thus of a very similar, kind may become the true subject of poetry. *Barbare* would seem to be as far as a poet can go in that direction for, although the work has lines of a powerful beauty, it does not have the authority, the sense of rightness, of a poem such as *Enfance*, and perhaps needs to be considered as some kind of failure. It is no more surprising that Rimbaud should have given up poetry than that Lautréamont (1846-1870) should have cast aside the style of *Les Chants de Maldoror* for the dull common sense of his final *Poésies*. However, giving up need not invalidate what has been done, even if Rimbaud came to consider his own writings disgusting, as he is said to have done. Also what has been written here implies no judgment upon modernist works as such, but merely points out that modernist attitudes are ones which tend to invite failure, even if they may lead to works, like the majority of Rimbaud's prose poems, which triumphantly avoid that.

Stéphane Mallarmé (1842-1898) certainly did not give up, and although his prose poems, unlike those of Rimbaud, can not be considered as his finest achievement,[13] his concern with language was of so profound a kind that the dilemma which the prose poem gives rise to can perhaps be seen more clearly in his work than elsewhere. This concern was (if simply stated) with the processes of language themselves rather than with what language is commonly supposed to point to, with artistic means rather than with ends, with the poetic revelation occurring in the very form of the language as it is used. All these attitudes have become truisms of modernist poetics, resulting in the expectation that the truly experimental work will not so much mean as simply be. However, no twentieth-century prose poet has gone as far as Mallarmé went in pursuing the implications of such ideas (this being what makes his case so instructive), for no prose since has achieved his wonderful rightness of phrase, combined with an obscurity of the prose work as a whole which eventually arrived at something perilously close to actual unreadability. This movement toward the opaque, the ungraspably abstract and, finally, toward what appears to be the very destruction of prose itself, can be seen in his prose poems. A look at them does, I believe, tell us more about the essence of modernism and the relationship it has to language than a consideration of the work of any other writer; since in Mallarmé this not only appears in its most brilliant, but also in its most extreme form.

Mallarmé's early prose poems were written so much under the influence of Baudelaire that one could accuse him of plagiarism in some of them,[14] and they show none of those profound concerns with "restructuring language," with language "shedding its object" in order to "reveal itself" which one finds in his later writings, as can be seen in this example, *La Pipe*.[15]

THE PIPE

Yesterday I came across my pipe while meditating a long evening's work, good winter work. My cigarettes cast aside with all the childish joys of summer, a past lit up with blue leaves in the sun, with muslins; and this grave pipe now taken up once more, by a serious man who wants to smoke a long time undisturbed, for that way one works better. But I had not foreseen what this abandoned object held in store for me; for hardly had I taken the first puff than I forgot the great books I should write, as wondering, as moved within, I breathed again last winter now come back.

I had not touched this faithful friend of mine since my return to France, and now the whole of London reappeared, London as I had lived it all within myself a year ago. First with the fogs I love which smother up the brain and have, those over there, an odor all their own as they seep through beneath the casement. My tobacco had the smell of a somber room, its leather chairs with their fine coating of coal dust, on which the thin black cat would roll. Then those enormous fires; the red-armed maid putting on more coals; and how they clattered down from the metal bucket into the iron scuttle, every morning, that moment when the postman beat his solemn double knock, a sound which each day made me live.

I saw again those sickly trees in the dusty square beyond my windows. And then the open sea, so often crossed that winter, shivering on the steamer's deck, soaked in the spray and black with smoke;—with my poor, wandering beloved, in her traveling clothes, a long dull dress the color of roadside dust, a cloak damply clinging to her cold shoulders, one of those feathered hats with so few ribbons, the kind which affluent ladies throw away as soon as they arrive, because they have been so savaged by the sea wind; but which a poor beloved must retrim for many seasons still to come.

Around her throat was wrapped that terrible handkerchief, the one we wave when saying goodbye for ever.

This is written in a prose of flowing elegance and no real obscurity, and also in a prose which observes the common law of the medium that it should be narrative in its structure and move toward an ending, achieving its final meaning in its final lines. This piece attains poetic status (if it does, for it is arguable that it does not, although I would not argue so) in its last sentence; and this

makes it similar to some of the prose poems of Inoue
Yasushi given in this volume, such as *The River Indus* on
page 152 or *The Evening Sun* on page 164.

Mallarmé wrote the above poem in 1864, when he was
twenty-two years old, the same year in which he announced in a letter to Henri Cazalis that he was inventing a new poetic language, which would paint, not the
thing itself but the effect it produced. This led to the famous crisis of 1866 onward, the "terrible vision of the
pure work"; in the prose writings from 1870 to 1875 one
can see all the characteristics of the mature Mallarméan
style coming into being, with almost no verse poems written again until into the 1880s. The outbreak of creative
energy around 1884 then led to a return to the prose poem
in 1885, and during the next two years produced some of a
very notable obscurity. The extract that follows, from *Le
Nénuphar Blanc*, is from the first and least obscure of
these, a work of real beauty, perhaps the finest prose
poem he ever wrote, but unfortunately not given in full
here because of its length. In the poem the poet has rowed
along a stream to the banks of the park of a lady whom he
is to meet, and has decided to depart before she should
appear. What follows are the closing paragraphs:

THE WHITE WATERLILY

....

Sum up within one look the virgin absence scattered
in this solitude and, as one gathers in memory of a
place one of those tight closed waterlilies which
suddenly arise, enfolding in their hollowed whiteness
nothing, a nothing made of thoughts intact, of
happiness that is never to take place, and of my breath
held in now with the fear of what would be a ghost; and
so depart with this; in silence, backing gently with the
oars, with no shock to break off illusion, nor plash of
any visible round of foam entangled in my flight, thus
casting at the feet of someone who might happen there
transparent likeness to the rape of my one ideal flower.

If, drawn by some sense there of the unforeseen, she had appeared, the thoughtful one, perhaps the proud, or the retiring or the gay; so much the worse then for that face now not to be described since it is never to be known. For I did the moves according to the book; got the boat free, swung round, and was already passing a slight bend in the stream, bearing away as my imaginary trophy a swan's noble egg from which no flight will ever burst, which swells with nothing but its own exquisite vacancy, and which in summer a lady will pursue, along the walks and pathways of her garden, as they all love to do, stopping often and at length, as if on the bank of a stream which must be crossed, or some expanse of water.

This poem is certainly anecdotal but, unlike the earlier work, it is about an event which does not take place, and seeming to realize Flaubert's dream of writing a work which would be about nothing. Again, the usual sequence of prose is still being observed, but each phrase seems to have discarded its normal referential function in a way difficult to analyze, for although the amount of reference to things which do not exist may have something to do with this, that explanation still does not tell one enough. This produces an effect of the language mainly revealing itself and not aiming at the traditional transparency of prose, an effect more powerfully received from the original than from this translation, and one at which the writer was clearly aiming. The question then is whether the physical sense of language can be allowed to dominate in this way if the reading habits which prose implies are still to be made use of; the real exhaustion which Mallarmé's prose on a subject such as fashion, for example, can induce in the reader, makes one feel that perhaps it should not. This is not only a question of obscurity, since those verse poems of his which are considerably more obscure than this one in prose do not arouse that kind of resistance. The liberation of the phrase, the word, requires a weight of attention set upon those words and phrases which the very arrangement of prose seems not to encourage. Either one breaks up that arrangement, as Rimbaud did, or one alienates the reader; as he surely must be alienated by the following example, *Reminiscence*.[16]

REMINISCENCE

Orphaned I wandered in black my eyes emptied of family. At the quincunx the tents of a fair were all spread out, and did I sense the future and that I would be thus, I loved the scent of vagabonds, forgetting my everyday friends while I was about them. No shout of choruses through the rent opening, nor far-off tirade, since the play requires the hour of footlights. I wished to talk to a kid too wobbly to take his place among the rest of his kind, wearing a nightcap like the hood of Dante; who was placing inside himself, in its aspect of a slice of bread and soft spread cheese, already the snow of the mountain tops, of lilies or of other whitenesses which would be constitutive of wings within there. I would have asked him to let me take part in this superior repast, so quickly shared with one of his famous seniors, suddenly appearing against a neighboring tent as he performed various powerful feats and other banalities pertaining to the day.

Naked to pirouette in the briskness of his tights surprising to my way of thinking he, moreover, began:
"Your parents?"
"I have none."
"Oh if you only knew how comic a father is.... Even the other week when he was off his food he went on making such faces that the ringmaster kept on thumping and kicking him," rejoicing in this by raising his leg with splendid ease; "Daddy really sends us," biting into the chaste feast of the very young.
"I guess you have no mother then; you are alone?

Mine eats oakum and everyone claps their hands. So you just don't know nothing you see, because parents are very comic people and they make you laugh a lot."

The parade was reaching a climax and he left; and I just sighed, suddenly feeling let down at not having parents.

Unfortunately the translation can not fully reproduce the obscure nature of the original; and yet, even so, the disturbing, perhaps even repellent, quality of the work perhaps comes through, and the fact that this is a rewriting of an original written in the same year as *La Pipe* allows one to see what has happened to his prose. If one compares it with that earlier version (since it shares the same characteristics as *La Pipe* a look at that work should show the same sort of thing) it is clear that the normal connections we expect of prose disappear as the whole is tightened up, with a greater use of abstract nouns and a cutting away of verbs. This means that the prose no longer *flows* in so far as its sequences of images and the overall movement of the meaning is concerned, although it still retains the normal rhythmic motion of prose, thus arousing expectations in the act of reading which tend to be frustrated. The reader who sympathizes with this still finds himself having to resist the rhythmic movement which the whole has, and set his concentration upon the existence of each phrase as it exists mysteriously by itself, and thus the revelation in the language itself is made. However, if this is to be done successfully, the eye itself needs assistance, and the typographical experiments of *Un Coup de Dés* are the natural outcome of this. How much any reading can ever be that kind of experience I do not know, but that the flow of prose resists it seems to be a fact, as the next extract makes more clear; the opening paragraphs (about one third of the whole) of *La Gloire*.

FAME

Fame! I only knew it yesterday, irrefragable, and nothing called thus by anyone will interest me.

A hundred posters assimilating in themselves the days' uncomprehended gold, betrayals of the word, have fled, as if to all the confines of the town, my eyes drawn flush with the horizon by a rail departure, before I recollect my thoughts in the abstruse pride the approach of a forest gives, with its period of apotheosis.

So discord in the excitement of the hour, a cry falsified this well-known name thus to deploy the continuity of these treetops disappeared of late, Fontainebleau, that I thought, the glass of the carriage door suffering violence, to seize the intruder's neck with my clenched fist too: Be quiet, you, do not divulge by the fact of your indifferent howling the shadow here insinuated in my spirit, to the carriage doors slammed by an inspired egalitarian wind, the omnipresent tourists vomited out.

This passage demonstrates how very precise and sensitive insights will not make their proper impact in a context of this kind. For example, the words "*l'abstruse fierté que donne une approche de forêt en son temps d'apothéose*" are wonderfully lucid about that sensation achieved when riding on a train which enters among trees. However, the words have to be brooded over before they reveal themselves, and prose does not allow us to do that unless it provides a context of truly prose-like clarity as a setting in which the non-prose insight can make sense. The poetic insight of almost every phrase in the work seems to me undeniable (after all, even "Be quiet, you, do not divulge by the fact of your indifferent howling the shadow here insinuated in my spirit," is very much the kind of thing one would like to say to a railway porter, only one never has the wit or nerve to do so). A whole series of them, however, becomes intolerable, since the static nature of each insight fails to create any continuing sense of overall insight. Thus each following insight tends to cancel out the one made before. The problem the prose poem must raise is that of whether poetic insight can truly be contained in prose contexts or not. The problem can only be ignored if one comes to believe, as Mallarmé did, that prose does not truly exist.

> Verse is everywhere in language where there is rhythm; everywhere, except in advertizements and on the fourth page of the newspapers. In the genre referred to as prose there are verses, sometimes admirable ones, of all kinds of rhythm. But, in truth, there is no prose: there is the alphabet, and then there is verse, more or less tightened, more or less diffuse. Every time there is an effort toward style, then there is versification.[17]

If one follows out the logic of what has been suggested above, it will appear that the prose poem is something poets should not write. However, legislative statements of that nature are as of little interest to poets as they should be to their readers, and it is no intention of mine to arrive at such, since the existence of this book would then be meaningless. What I have wished to provide is a context in which the reader can think over the relationship between poetic statement and prose form, and be reminded how much modernism entails some kind of assault upon traditional concepts of the function of language. A form as essentially paradoxical as the poem in prose encourages a consciousness of these linguistic questions on the part of both poet and reader, thus making this form the logical choice for any poet who accepts what modernism implies (although he obviously has other choices too). The lack of prose poems in English literature (there are some, but there is nothing like the French tradition I have outlined) indicates how little the literatures written in that language have truly responded to modernist poetics. This point needs to be stressed because a reader of English may well be unsympathetic to much modern Japanese poetry, because it is in that tradition his own literature has never fully accepted; and yet any reader of translations must start out with more sympathy than he need give to writings in his own language or he will never make the imaginative leap required to arrive somewhere near the original, at which the translation can only point. My occasional expressions of doubt about the modernist venture as it appears in the prose poem have been an attempt to make the reader conscious of such doubts within himself. However, I have also wished to stress that this need not prevent him from recognizing, and responding to, the value of the literature which has come out of that tradition, for the greatness of the three French poets dealt with here is beyond question. When I ask the reader to "sympathize" I am not demanding any misplaced enthusiasm, but only a willingness to see things as they are. A few more pages about the six poets translated here and their relationship to this literary genre are now required, then the reader should be prepared to read the poems themselves.

If one ignores the prose poems of the *Minshūha* (Democratic group) as not properly related to the genre being dealt with, then the first modern Japanese prose poems are those of Hagiwara Sakutarō (1889-1942). These were brought together quite late in his life (in *Shukumei* [*Fate*], 1935), although many of them had been published earlier in two volumes of aphorisms. In his preface[18] to the 1935 volume Hagiwara wrote that the founder of this form in the West was normally considered to be Baudelaire, who had discarded fixed metric form, so that the poem could be written freely as prose while still maintaining a high degree of musical rhythm and a strong "poetic aura." In Japan the "free poem" (*vers libre*) was really this same kind of poem, although the poem in prose ought to be a different species of composition; this difference being, he presumed, mainly one of content. The prose poem should naturally stress ideas more than the pure lyric did, its content being philosophical rather than imaginative.

Hagiwara admitted that few of his own prose poems, perhaps only four or five, were really poems at all.[19] Among these four of five he included the following, for he had spent a great deal of trouble over its rhythmical and melodic aspects: *Kyomu no Uta*.[20]

THE SONG OF NOTHINGNESS

Three o'clock in the afternoon. In the middle of a vast hall I am drinking beer alone. There are no other customers, nor any sign even of anything moving. The stove burns bright, and through the thick glass doors comes piercing in the sad light of late afternoon. White concrete floor, tables which seem to have no place there, numerous thin legs of chairs.

Why have I come to this dismal beer hall near the bridge at Ebisu? What am I waiting here for? I am waiting for no mistress, for no passion, hope, nor for good fortune. When I was young I had a passion for all things. But now, already old and tired, I have lost all that. I had been roaming the streets of the town, looking for a chair to be alone in. Because I knew what I was looking for; for a free space in time in which to drink cold beer and look upon the clouds. All I have really searched for from way back has been just this.

Before I used to think about the spirit, the single will to dream, morality warm as blood, the trembling of the thinking reed, the yearning for the void, heart-rending prayers to Eros. But then the spirit was really this, all these remembrances that I have lost. Before I used to think about the body, this wretched thing formed out of cells and matter, which hungers, reproduces, fights unendingly with inorganic things which strive on always for its dissolution; suffering piteously all its life, this miserable thing which breathes like a shellfish. Ah, but that is all far from me now, becoming just remembrance of the past. For I am old, have lost the warmth for all fleshly desires. Graves, stones, and toads wait underground for me.

Out in the yard a paulownia grows, scattering its dead leaves on the ground. Beyond the fence surrounding it an area of waste ground and storehouses, before which no one passes. Vague chimneys float up in the sky; a far crowd of children's voices seem like something in a dream. Birds whistle sometimes in the wide, deserted hall. Afternoon in late autumn; three o'clock; near the bridge at Ebisu. White concrete floor, tables which seem to have no place there, numerous thin legs of chairs.

Ah God! There is no way to get things back. I have lost all now, everything. And yet even now what happiness it would be, if I could but believe, if I could but believe that I still live, and would go on in living, would still be. If I could but believe that some external nothing would remain eternally within me. God, let me believe in that until the end of all my empty days.

If that were so, then I should have lost nothing in my past, and now there would be nothing I had lost. So absentmindedly, almost a man who has maybe lost his mind, I look up at the sky, content with what is my own happiness; which is to sit, today and yesterday, and drink this peaceful, marvelous beer. Ah nothingness! Ah clouds! Ah life!

Hagiwara went on to explain in his note on this poem that he had tried as far as possible to approach the Baudelairean concept of musicality without meter in the prose poem, but that he had managed to do so only to a slight extent. Unlike the lyrical poem, he added, the poem depended upon intellectual and conceptual elements, and since traditional Japanese had been so meager in its philosophical vocabulary, such terminology (from Western sources, presumably, although he does not say so specifically) will not fit in with the spirit of the Japanese language. He felt that the attempt to write intellectually in Japanese only led to a tasteless, dry, academic form of language, but also that the avoidance of that resulted in merely impressionistic sequences with no true rhythm running through them. As long as one wrote in Japanese the artistic prose poem of Baudelaire must remain an impossibility.

Although this difficulty about how to give an intellectual content to the poem is one perhaps every modern Japanese poet has met, these remarks of Hagiwara's only show how far he was from sharing the modernist view of the poem in prose. Indeed, this "impressionistic sequence with no rhythm running through it" which he feared Japanese poetry had to be is, in fact, much closer to that tradition than the above prose poem of his. Also that remark of his is probably an indication of his lack of sympathy with the New Prose Poem Movement, since this preface was written some time after that movement had come to an end. Those poets, however, had not seen this impressionistic sequence as something the Japanese past had condemned them to write, but rather as the form in which the poetry of the future should be.

The selection from Miyoshi Tatsuji (1900-1964) is given before that of Anzai Fuyue (1898-1965), despite the fact that Anzai's work appeared a year earlier than Miyoshi's *Sokuryōsen (The Survey Ship)*, 1930, since his poems are closer to that Japanese past than the undoubtedly modernist writings of Anzai. Miyoshi is one of the few modern Japanese poets to have been read widely by the Japanese public, and this volume has been a part of that popularity even if the best-liked poems in it have been the ones in free verse. However, more than two-thirds of the book consisted of prose poems, and Miyoshi's later rejection of it as a mistaken path taken in his youth, suggests that for him it was much more an experimental, modernist venture than his readers seem to have read it as. After this volume Miyoshi returned to the literary language and the lyrical tradition, in which he wrote some of the finest poems in Japanese of this century. However, even in his short modernist period he does not seem far away from that tradition, and it is for this reason that his poems have been placed first.

In an interview published in July 1927 in the magazine *Shii no ki* (*The Oak Tree*) Miyoshi said that he was gradually finding it difficult to accept the kind of line divisions found in the normal free verse poem. Consequently he had chosen the prose poem as an alternative, although he still wanted the resulting prose to be read slowly, so that its poetic meanings would be clear. In comments elsewhere on the poems in this first volume he stressed the simplicity of what he had been trying to do, and the kind of *haiku*-like structure and insight aimed at should be plain to the reader. The poems are, in fact, a reaction against the free-verse poem, rather than any truly modernist attempt. The closeness to traditional modes can be seen in the fact that there are two "prose poems" which are *haibun* (*haiku* set within a descriptive, elegant prose) written in the literary language. I should have liked to give an example of one of these, but it was beyond my powers to create two forms of English prose which would show something of the difference between the two kinds of Japanese. It seems fair to say that Miyoshi's modernism was little more than an interest in French literature, a concern with visual rather than with rhythmic values, and a reaction against the prolix colloquial poems of the Democratic group. Miyoshi's favorite volume of French poetry was Verlaine's *Sagesse*,[21] and in the ambiguous relationship that work has to the French symbolist/modernist tradition one can see something very similar to the position of this volume by Miyoshi.

Even so, Miyoshi was a leading figure in the group of poets who collected around the magazine *A*, which Anzai edited in Manchuria from 1924 to 1927, the precursor to the already mentioned *Poetry and Poetics*. Anzai's *Gunkan Mari* (*The Warship Mari*) was published in 1929, and included a number of single-line poems, although most of it consisted of poems in prose. The "Short Poem Movement" had preceded the "New Prose Poem Movement," but since the same poets were involved in both they can be considered as essentially the same movement, a reaction against the prosaicisms of the Democratic poets. This movement toward brevity is an aspect of modernism anywhere. Anzai is perhaps better known to literary history for these single line poems, the following being the most famous of them, *Haru* ("Spring").

> One butterfly passed over the Tartar Straits.

A poem of this kind defies translation much as the *haiku* does. In the original there is a marked contrast between the fragile-looking, almost dancing *kana* (phonetic) letters used for "butterfly" and the complex fierceness of the *kanji* (ideograms) used for "Tartar," for the setting together of these two conflicting aspects of reality is what the poem is about. Even so, the reader will feel the closeness of this to what he imagines the *haiku* tradition to be, since the *haiku* is also a "single-line poem" even if the tradition of English translation usually presents it as a tercet. He would not be wrong in this feeling, although the poem is most certainly not a modern *haiku* since it makes use of that tradition only in order to show how it refuses to belong to it. The fact that the literary language is not used is what the poem stresses by using old-fashioned *kana* to write the word "butterfly," and the objects the poem is about carry none of the referential values traditionally associated with them. Anzai is refusing to be allusive in the way that Bashō, for example, constantly is, and this is what is new in his poem. His "butterfly" is in the Western symbolist tradition which, in its modernist form, has tried to free itself from any specific, allegorical connotations. In this next poem, *Jūnen* (Ten Years), the absence of any traditional reference is even more clear.

> Ten years. A world like white porcelain dice.
> Purity filthier than filth.

This is a poem which makes only personal references, having no contact with any tradition but only with the world of language which is, as it were, being deprived of its history here as the poet tries to give us back that real history to which our traditions and customs have, presumably, made us insensitive. Since the poem has such aims, then it must be called a modernist poem.

Much modernism of this kind in Japan in the 1920's has been strongly criticized by the Japanese themselves, a value judgment I have no right to go against. However, it also seems unquestionable that Anzai's poems have an energy which puts them beyond the accusations of shallow imitation leveled at that literature. This may well be because, as Kitagawa Fuyuhiko pointed out in his original preface to *The Warship Mari*, Anzai's literature is "a literature of consolation."[22] As a young man Anzai had his right lower leg amputated, and his attempts to create a poetic world deprived of the past have a clear counterpart in his personal needs. Thus the poems attain a life rare in a phase of Japanese literature when writers seemed more concerned with absorbing French modernism, rather than with discovering what the Japanese kind should really be. One of the things this book also shows is how shallow the roots of modernism in Japan were at this time; the tough line in sensibility which the hard surface of the language implies is often broken down by a warm, traditional sentimentalism; a tendency which grows as the book proceeds. Something of the same can be seen in Miyoshi, but in his case he seems to welcome it, whereas Anzai's poetic effort is essentially against this emotional sensibility. The tension produced at times by this half-acceptance of an emotionalism his poetry should constantly reject may well be closer to the energy of neurosis than of art, although one could argue either way, and even reject the distinction itself. However, the fragmented images, the lack of rhythmic pattern in the prose, the slipping away into ironic attitudes when the emotion looks as though it were becoming too strong; all these are so clearly related to the modernist prose-poem/free-verse tradition that there is perhaps no real need to point them out.

The prose poems of Tamura Ryūichi (1923–) and Yoshioka Minoru (1919–) are in a form which had been used slightly before the Pacific war, becoming the standard one after it. The fact that the prose is broken up into fragments with no punctuation (the shape this takes in English is a fair indication of what the original is like) is a clear denial of the normal continuity of prose. This means there can be backward references within the poem since it does not move forward in the accepted way, and the poem can be difficult to grasp. In this respect Tamura does not provide the same degree of difficulty as Yoshioka, since Tamura's poems still have a narrative movement of a kind which Yoshioka consistently avoids.

The poems translated here are all the prose poems in both Tamura's *Yonsen no hi to yoru* (*Four thousand days and nights*), 1956 and Yoshioka's *Sōryo* (*The Priests*), 1958, perhaps still the volumes by which these poets are best known. Tamura has written almost no prose poems since these, and Yoshioka, although his next volume contained some, has also devoted himself to the free-verse form; a form in which both of them have written their best work, which is arguably the finest poetry written in postwar Japan. Even so, the writing of the prose poem has obviously been of importance for both, for Tamura has said that the first poem in which he finally achieved the kind of thing he wanted to write was the prose poem "Etching,"[23] and one could say that Yoshioka first found himself in his prose poems as well. Here one sees the anti-traditional meaning the prose poem can have for the Japanese poet, and the fact that neither has persisted with it indicates how such conscious anti-traditionalism is not an attitude any Japanese poet can feel comfortable in for very long.

Tanikawa Shuntarō (1931–) appeared on the literary scene in 1952 with a volume of free-verse poems of a surrealist kind which have been variously translated into English. He has written the same kind of fragmented prose poem as that of Tamura and Yoshioka, but has also shown an interest in quite normal prose of an almost old-fashioned descriptive kind, although the volume *Teigi (Definitions)*, 1975, from which the poems translated here have been taken, is not of that kind. It shows rather what the prose poem will become if the logic of the form is fully worked out. To combine poetic structure with the normal flow of prose means that the prose movement will tend to become a circular one, one which keeps turning back upon itself. This is also what a definition has to be even in its most extended form. If poetic statements are to be made in prose, one must either break up the prose rhythm, as in Yoshioka, or allow it to keep on creating the same pattern. In either case a sense of stasis is created, which the poem requires and prose normally rejects. Tanikawa's attitude toward what he is doing shares that ambivalence which often marks modernist writing (the first poem translated here is a fine example of this). Also the first poem in the Japanese volume (not translated here) is a passage taken straight from an encyclopedia, an attempt to raise a similar skepticism in the reader about what kind of construct the poem is.

French modernism can now be seen as a continuation of a literary tradition extending back through symbolism to romanticism. The desire to go against traditional concepts of language and literary form is only the most extreme aspect of a richer and more complex view of literature than I have stressed here. Japanese modernism is, however, essentially a break with the past, not a continuation of anything. That heroic desire to go it alone which marks Japanese modernism in the 1920s has now become, it seems, an unavoidable fate since, as Ōoka Makoto (himself a poet) has pertinently said, the colloquial-language poem has never created a tradition and each new poet must make a totally new start.[24]

The French language has not made the same break with the past, not even with its literary past, let alone its linguistic one. It is the persistence of the alexandrine which marks so much poetry in free verse in this century, a form which continually turns up in Breton and Eluard. This frequency has been conveniently counted in the case of Aragon, the result being that in an analysis of two thousand lines the alexandrine totaled 30.5 percent of all, whereas actual free verse made up only a meager 18 percent.[25] The Japanese fives and sevens have never been a verse form of that kind and, although that rhythm may sometimes slip into the language any Japanese poet now uses, it is hardly noticeable in comparison with what is not there, the whole system of language in which Japanese poems have been written for over a thousand years. The reader who senses an emptiness in some of these poems should understand the reason why such emptiness might be there.

A concept such as "emptiness" can always be thought of in more positive terms as "sparseness" or "bareness," and does not have to be a failing in art. It is still not possible to judge whether what has happened to the Japanese used in poetry can be considered as good or bad, or as neither. Nobody would wish to argue that what happened to English poetry in the sixteenth century was a disaster because it ceased to use the language of Chaucer, and because the blank-verse line was established under strong foreign influence. A similar caution is required in the case of Japanese poetry in this century. A poetic tradition is a number of poems, and no matter how important one may consider the rationalization of the existence of those poems, an over-emphasis upon the fact or non-fact of a tradition may blind one to the only things that really matter, the poems themselves. However, it is also true that the Japanese language in its modern form has created a tradition of writing in the prose novel as it has not done in the case of the poem. The last poet in this selection belongs more to that prose tradition than to the poetic one for, although Inoue's are still prose *poems* their language relates more to what prose is than to what poetry has become in present-day Japan.

Inoue Yasushi (1907–) is a successful novelist, some of whose work is available in English translation. In the afterword to his first book of prose poems, *Hokkoku* (*The North Country*), 1958, he said that he considered his poems not as actual poetry, but as convenient containers created in order that the "poems" he experienced should not escape entirely. The true act of poetry, he felt, required an incantatory form of language of which he was not capable.[26] Indeed the language of his prose poems is very much that of his novels, and if they become poems they do so by fact of their structure. Inoue's use of such prose means that his writing has a more direct connection with traditional modes of thought and feeling than most postwar poetry has, a fact in itself neither good nor bad. The poems given here date from as early as 1946 to as late as 1976, the extraordinary continuity of the style (extraordinary if compared with most twentieth-century Japanese poets) implies that he is writing comfortably in a tradition which does not seem to make any demand upon him to change. If Tanikawa's style over the same period reminds one of all the interesting things that have happened to plastics over the past thirty years, then Inoue's will seem like the unchanging earth. There is nothing, however, on *a priori* grounds, which makes one prefer earth to plastic or plastic to earth, since both are now a true part of our lives.

The reader has perhaps already grasped what kind of translations he is being asked to read, by way of the examples given from the French. If he compares the versions of Baudelaire here with the same works as translated by Norman Cameron,[27] for example, he will notice that I have tried to achieve a stronger rhythm, the desire to do so having sometimes affected the vocabulary choices. However, these are still, in effect, literal translations, as are Norman Cameron's. I stress this point because it is not difficult to come across translations of modern Japanese poetry which are nothing of the kind, being bold attempts to recreate the essence of the original. Although there must be reasons for translating in that way or, presumably, people would not do so, I have assumed the Japanese poet to have a better understanding of what he was up to than I have myself. Thus each poem has been translated in as literal a manner as the differences between the two languages will allow. I have still tried to create a stronger rhythm than others might think was proper, because I think that poetic meaning in English requires such a rhythm if it is to exist at all. This is an opinion in which I am aware I may be mistaken, so it seems important to state it openly.

This does not mean that I have not at times felt obliged to take slight liberties with the original, but I have not done this on principle, and I have always done it for the specific reason of making something clear which otherwise would not have been so. I do not believe that a reader of a translation expects to find the same sort of thing he experiences when reading poems in his own language. What he requires is the sense that he is close to the original, yet in a form of his own language which does not offend his idea of what poetic statement demands. It is that kind of expectation I have tried to respond to here.

There have been occasions when I have had to do otherwise, sometimes because the result sounded all wrong, but usually for some particular reason of meaning. For example, in the poem *Enfance Finie* by Miyoshi

Tatsuji, I have translated the phrase "*Aa aware na watashi yo*" ("Oh, wretched me") as "Grief." In this case "Oh, wretched me" would be comic in a way that the Japanese is not, since the Japanese are more tolerant of statements of that kind that English readers have become. The word "grief" was chosen because the original has a word very close to that in meaning, because its French overtones seemed right for the context, and also because, although Japanese readers are more tolerant of such expressions of self-pity than we may be, they are still not totally tolerant of them. A Japanese reader who is not in tune with the poem at that point will snigger or groan over it, and such an opportunity is offered in the translation. There is a limit to how much a translator can squeeze out of his head, and a more precise translation was beyond me.

Again, in the poem "Sunflowers are already black gunpowder" by Anzai Fuyue, the remark about "WeWeWeWeWeWeWe" looking like children skipping is much less intelligible than the original. The two *kana* letters "*wa*" and "*re*" in "*ware ware*" ("we") do in fact look, if one looks closely, like the upswing and downswing of a skipping-rope. "We" does not look like that; an awkward-minded person might argue that "W" has a sense of raised arms about it, and "e" the swaying circularity of the skipping-rope, but he would have to be joking. However, since no other member of the alphabet provides much assistance it seemed more important to retain the semantic value of "we" rather than search for the unfindable. The main meaning of that line in the context of the poem lies in its light yet moving lack of consequentiality; since that still remains I felt no great loss had resulted. Obviously this kind of verbal play is going to disappear in translation, although the reader should still be allowed to sense its existence. If one tries too hard to retain it (as may have happened in the first poem of Tanikawa's given here), the result can have an awkwardness it should not have, since verbal play really ought to be playful.

Finally, there have been a very few cases in which some expansion of the original was required in order to get the meaning across. The most striking example of this is in Inoue's "Old man in a turban," where two Chinese names, which would mean nothing to any but the most informed reader, have been glossed so that they should make sense. This has created a dignity in the translation which goes against the bare statement of the original, but the plain statement of important names can create a similar sense for a reader who belongs to that culture, and thus it seemed forgivable. The form this worked-in gloss took was again conditioned by what seemed to me the rhythmic demands of the surrounding English, and by those of the poetic matter being put forward in the prose form. Where I have offended against the literal requirements that any poem has made, it has been mainly for such reasons.

NOTES TO THE INTRODUCTION

1. An example of one of these can be found in F. J. Daniels, ed., *Selections from Japanese Literature*, Lund Humphries, London, 1958, pp. 52-59 and 146-149. Examples of the Chinese *Fu* can be found in any good anthology, but the definitive work is Burton Watson, trans., *Chinese Rhyme Prose, Poems in the Fu form from the Han and Six Dynasties Period*, Columbia University Press, New York, 1971.

2. Suzanne Bernard, *Le Poème en Prose, de Baudelaire jusqu'à nos Jours*, Librairie Nizet, Paris, 1959, p. 23.

3. *Ibid.*, pp. 24-28.

4. *Ibid.*, pp. 39-43.

5. See Murano, *et al.*, eds., *Kōza, Nihon Gendaishi Shi*, 4 vols., Ubun Shoin, Tokyo, 1973, vol. I, cap. one *passim*.

6. 'Nōzui Nikki' in *Nishiwaki Junzaburō Zenshū*, ten vols., Chikuma Shobō, Tokyo, 1971, v. 328-344.

7. 'Shinsanbunshi e no michi', *Shi to Shiron*, No. 3, 1929.

8. See Bernard, *op.cit.*, p. 61, for an example of this.

9. In Francis Scarfe, ed., *Baudelaire, Selected Verse*, Penguin, Harmondsworth, 1961, pp. 57-58. "A Hemisphere in Your Hair" is on pp. 59-60 of the same volume.

10. See Michael Hamburger, *The Truth of Poetry*, Penguin, Harmondsworth, 1972, p. 6.

11. See Scarfe, pp. 232-234 and 248-251 for all three poems.

12. There is an English translation of *Le Peintre de la Vie Moderne* in Peter Quennell, ed., *Charles Baudelaire, The Essence of Laughter*, Meridian Books, New York, 1956, pp. 19-62. The same volume also gives translations of some of the prose poems, notebooks, and journals.

13. Judy Kravis, *The Prose of Mallarmé, The Evolution of a Literary Language*, Cambridge University Press, Cambridge, 1976, devotes only six out of 232 pages on the above subject to the prose poems.

14. See Bernard, p. 257.

15. The originals of all the Mallarmé poems can be found in either Anthony Hartley, *Mallarmé*, or Keith Bosley, *Mallarmé: The Poems*, which both provide reliable translations; both are from Penguin, the former in 1965 and the latter in 1977.

16. "One is obliged to admit that these final prose poems (I am thinking in particular of *Reminiscence* and *The Traveling Declaration*) are such as to nonplus even sympathetic readers." Bernard, p. 309. On p. 307 she gives an analysis of the changes made between this later and the earlier version.

17. From an interview in 1891. See Stéphane Mallarmé, *Igitur, Divagations, Un coup de dés*, Gallimard, Paris, 1976, p. 389.

18. *Hagiwara Sakutarō Zenshū*, Shinchōsha, Tokyo, 1959, 5 vols., I, 391-392.

19. *Ibid.*, p. 468.

20. *Ibid.*, p. 439.

21. See Kitagawa Fuyuhiko, *Gendaishi Kanshō*, 2 vols., Yushindō, Tokyo, 1970, II, 51.

22. *Gendaishishū*, Chikuma Shobō, Tokyo, 1973, p. 18.

23. *Tamura Ryūichi Shishū*, Shichōsha, Tokyo, 1968, p. 91.

24. Ooka Makoto, *Tōji no Kakei*, Shichōsha, Tokyo, 1975, pp. 18-20.

25. W. K. Wimsatt, ed., *Versification: Major Language Types*, New York University Press, New York, 1972, p. 188.

26. Inoue Yasushi, *Hokkoku*, Shinchō Bunko, Tokyo, 1960, p. 90.

27. In Quennell, *op. cit.*, note 12.

BIBLIOGRAPHICAL NOTE

The text used for the poems by Miyoshi Tatsuji has been *Miyoshi Tatsuji Zenshū*, Chikuma Shobō, Tokyo, 1964, vol. i; and that for those of Anzai Fuyue, Tamura Ryūichi and Yoshioka Minoru is *Gendaishishū*, Chikuma Shobō, Tokyo, 1973. Tanikawa Shuntarō's *Teigi* was published by Shichōsha, Tokyo, in 1975. The first two of Inoue Yasushi's volumes can be found in *Inoue Yasushi Bunko*, Shichōsha, Tokyo, 1963, xxvi. 28-149. The other three volumes were published by Chikuma Shobō (*Unga*) in 1967, Kōdansha (*Kisetsu*) in 1971, and Shūeisha (*Enseiro*) in 1976, all in Tokyo. *Hokkoku* also appears in paperback from *Shinchō Bunko*, Tokyo, 1960.

The penguin editions of Baudelaire, Rimbaud, and Mallarmé referred to in the Notes to the Introduction (nos. 9 and 15) are recommended since they provide translations as well as the original text. Since all the prose poems I have translated do not occur in the penguin *Baudelaire*, it can be supplemented by the Norman Cameron translations in The *Essence of Laughter* (note no. 12). The authoritative work on the French prose poem is that by Dr. Suzanne Bernard (note no. 2), to which I am considerably indebted.

Quite a lot of modern Japanese poetry has been translated into English, although it is not easy to get hold of. Rimer and Morell, eds., *Guide to Japanese Poetry*, give information on this, as well as a general account of Japanese poetry (G. K. Hall & Co., Boston, 1975). Donald Keene, *Landscapes and Portraits*, Kodansha International, Tokyo and Palo Alto, 1971, pp. 131-156, gives an account of early modern Japanese poetry.

MIYOSHI TATSUJI

Echo
The Village
Spring
Village
The Pass
A Town
The Garden
Garden
Noon
Memoire
Enfance Finie
The Pheasant
Among the Branches

Echo

Evening gathered in; clouds like a blue-grey map of the world hung poised on the horizon.

He stood in the fields where the wind moved only the leaves of grass, and in a high-pitched voice called after his mother.

People in the town would laugh at him, because his face was so like hers. Which way had she gone, back bent like a fishhook, step by step, leaving her footprints behind her? The white road rose up clear in the dusk, and he called after her; sending his high-pitched shout into its distance.

So then what quietly reached his ear, was it the echo of his cry, or that of his mother far off calling after her own?

Evening gathered in; blue-grey clouds hung poised on the horizon.

The Village

They had tied up the deer by the antlers with a straw rope, and put her in the dark barn. Her blue eyes shone where nothing could be seen; and there she sat, neatly, elegantly. One potato tumbled down.

Outside the cherry blossoms fell, and a bicycle came down the hill, laying one long, clear line of them.

You saw the back of a little girl peering among the bushes. She had a black ribbon fixed to the shoulder of her dress.

Spring

Geese: So many of us together that each cries out in order not to mislay himself.

Lizard: No matter what stone I crawl upon, my belly stays cold.

Village

With wide eyes open glittering in fear the deer was already dead. It lay under the eaves of the lumber shed, the face of an awkward quarrelsome boy who refuses to say one word, soaked in an evening drizzle of rain. This one had been killed by dogs. In the bluish-black gloss of its fur the wounds on the thigh were red, more than camellia-red. The legs poked stiffly out like sticks, and the soft vague fur of its hindquarters was sodden with water, shameful.

The scent of onions drifted here from somewhere.

Wild flowers bloomed;* the water wheel turning behind the shed made its huge circles.

*Edgworthia Chrysantha

The Pass

I sat at the high point of the pass.

This small and nameless pass was overgrown with shrub, with trees, lost and hidden in thick reed grass. I smoked a cigarette and then the six or seven miles still to go became finally real to me, as if exposed to view in all that undergrowth.

In the last village I had passed they told me that the people of the fishing village I was on my way to used to climb this pass each morning to sell their fish; but with the coming of diesel-powered boats they had switched their market to across the bay. So far I had not come across one person on my way up here.

The path was now a wilderness, washed away by the rains and seemingly winding between the gorse and the tall pampas grass, and it was easy to lose one's way. In the trees on both sides of the path wood doves were cooing.

The sky was clear. Far off, through a gap in the bushes, you could see a number of grassy hills caught in the full light of the sun, and then, much farther off beyond their smooth and undulating shapes, the mountain, misted in deep indigo, which occupied the sky.

The blankness in my mind, the mild exhaustion sensed on looking at those hills, felt consolation in the autumn sunlight. And then I heard, coming it seemed from somewhere far away among those hills and hollows in some place I could not see, or even perhaps on the slopes there of the mountain, the muffled thud of a ship's engine. It seemed to go on for some moments and, as I could not believe my ears, I strained to hear more clearly; then once more all again was still with nothing to be heard. The wind occasionally stirred the bushes as it passed; or a bee hummed among them and its drone died out, then in curved flight appeared again from somewhere. Above, the soft beat of the white wings of the swallows fluttered down the air.

And then I thought how there were other passes like this one among those hills I could not see; there, perhaps, on the top of that ridge there, and elsewhere, and all like this, exactly like, all small and hidden away. And there also in all of them the wind was blowing, the bees and swallows flew; and there too I was sitting just as here. So as I gazed upon the scattered small white wildflowers at my feet, I felt that I could know them too, those other passes, so many of them covered and hidden away from me.

I carefully stubbed out my cigarette. The afternoon had started to grow late. I thought of this road I must go and where I would meet no one, the unknown downward path deep in thick grass; and of my freedom here, the freedom of a bird far from all men; and this free space of time became a weariness, a blankness for me, and I hastened to be on my way.

How many days had I already spent in travel; for I felt a sorrow in me like a sickness at the thought. Yet I should feel as men of old had done, traveling the roads, entrusting themselves to what they saw about them, singing the endless passing of the seasons. I knew I soon would look upon the sea, and yet what pain can autumn set about the heart.

Ah that village by the shore, hearing the pine trees murmur in the wind; the inn there with its gloomy bathroom, the window which looks out upon the bay. I wanted to lie soaking there before the sun went down beyond its headland.

So I heard the break and flow of waves within me, and went on down the pass.

A Town*

In this hollow among the mountains, this cruel waste; on what seems a heap of broken plates a small town offers itself, like one prayer, to the sky. A square held in by walls, breastwork which crumbles silently each night, and falls.

By all four walls are rows of willow trees, thick branched, throwing the shadows of long centuries gone. Even now a rustling storm of wings beat down, and pale white cranes fly over.

At noon out from the gate they burst, honking and squealing, running, tumbling, a line of black emaciated pigs, eagerly racing to the open fields, to disappear amid the shrubs and grasses. And if you hear far-off at times, coming from the shadow of the trees, an odd, melancholy creaking sound, then you will see, dragged by a mountainous red ox, a tiny two-wheeled cart, piled in summer with melons, loaded in autumn with firewood, moving toward the entrance of the town.

The wood of the main gate is blackened and peeled with age, and, in its lattice, shield-shaped cage now open to the sky, the bell hangs small and silent, forgetful that it ever tolled; the dignity of centuries of silence raised high up to the vaulted ceiling.

Magpies gather on the crumbling walls, upon the rubble of them; they gather on the trailing, whitening, uncut willows; flutter there, spreading long white-spotted tails; and screeching all day long in cries that rap against the rocks.

*In North Korea where Miyoshi was stationed for a year or so as a young military cadet.

But then beyond all this, when sometimes the waxing moon raises its faint half-circle over the far-scattered fields, over the corn and millet, over the bone-like range of mountains, one far point in the sky at noon; then do they feel the blankness of this land which covers them in waves, desolate knowledge that they have been set apart, knowing no touch of civilized life? In that full moment of awareness do they weep, bewail their solitary, outcast lot? Columns of smoke, at times how many, making the desolation yet more deep, from cooking fires drift up in the sky.

Long ago did their ancestors come one way through the mountains here to build this town? Then, on the very day the work was done, did enemies come down from the opposite direction? These breastworks were the scene for violent war then, the boundary line between them? So history forgot as they forgot, ceasing to care, solely following never-changing custom; eating their yellowish food from the same utensils, scattering the same seed in the plains, wrapping the same clothes about them. The same crown handed down was always set on similarly styled hair.

Perhaps their indolence, too, comes from decree; sleeping at all hours, rising in the intervals of dreams; and swelling their thick chests, gulping down huge quantities of water, because the air which flows through here is parched and dry.

Finally, when night falls, will this town go under, a coral reef under the rising tide, drowning in the pressure of this silence, sinking beneath such heavy darkness? What lights will they raise then and in what vessels? Perhaps they have no need for light? I do not know. I stand now on a road back through past time, looking down on that town, distant, recalled. But all my memories turn from there, ever hurrying back to where the sun is sinking.

The Garden

    The sun was still blocked by the dark storehouse, and the frosted garden lay deep in its long, cold, purple shadow. That morning I picked up the corpse of a crow which had frozen to death. The obdurate wings were folded spindle-shape, gray eyelids firmly closed. When I threw it away it fell on the lawn with an empty thud. I looked closer; blood was oozing slowly from it.

    Elsewhere in the clear sky I could hear a crow still calling.

Garden

    The shadow of the pagoda tree showed me the place, so I swung my pickaxe hard into the turf. Five minutes of leisurely digging and I dug it up; a skull clogged in earth. I took it to the pond and washed it. I should have been more careful and so not scored a hole in its temple as I dug, which I regretted now. I went back to my room and put it under the bed.

    That afternoon I went down the valley to shoot pheasants. When I got back I noticed a trail of water around one of the legs of the bed. That weighty toy I'd dug up had been wet, and now the sockets of its eyes and that scarred hole still were. And small red ants went running in and out, in and out of their pale brown, oddly magnificent fortress.

    A letter came from mother. I wrote an answer to it.

Noon

Parting feels other than it should; strangely like the first meeting with a girl, hurried and confused with bitter-tasting undertones. A studied cheerfulness, bright courage for the one who leaves; while he who stays behind puffs at his useless cigarette, at sudden moments sensing a slight absurdity in this.

The coach took her, her small wicker trunk and two wrapped bundles, and went straight off into the distance. The sunlight through the trees flickered across its pale-blue curtains, the horse-shoe patterns flashing like trout in water. Suddenly all, horses, coachman, seemed to have been just set loose in the world, birds now with no place to go. Goodbye, goodbye; the light-blue window of her room stays open as it was.

The road follows the river, avenues of trees through fields. The coach has gone behind that curve now, far off in the hills. Soon they will reach the bridge, the white one you can't see from here, cross over as the planks resound and clatter, sounds which will reach to where we are.

Noon now, everything is clear and blue. A column of bantam hens strut by the wall.

To think that time can thus be seen so clearly.

Feeling alone I bought myself a red apple.

Memoire

    My sister died in the autumn wind. I tried picking her white bones up out of the ash, but they kept breaking. The oven they burned her in was warm. All round about the autumn wind kept turning. I placed my lips and tongue to the cheek of her child. Then I set out on a journey. Infrequent letters from my love had ceased to come. The sea was clear: the sky was blue. At that time I was reading Aristotle. A battleship was anchored off the coast. You heard the bugle calls at dusk. Then again the lights came on. Some ceremony taking place up on the mountain. I walked a long way between fields of rice. Then a long flight of ancient steps among the trees. You see it was a long way up that mountain. I drank there; I poured wine.

Enfance Finie

    Islands far out at sea . . . camellia flowers fallen in the rain. Spring visits the bird cage, a bird cage where there is no bird.

    It seems that we have reached an end of promises.

    Yes, there are clouds over the sea and, yes, the earth reflects within those clouds.

    There is a stairway in the sky.

    Lower the flag of ceremony then, and say goodbye; flow like the great river. My footprints on this floor; a light dust on my footprints. Grief.

    Leave then now, then leave; set out on far journeys.

The Pheasant

On the mountainside magnolia trees stand white. A flock of crows alight in the field of reeds. A crow then looks at me. I look far off to the mountain where a narrowing line of telegraph poles goes over. I hide among the folds in the mountain's side.

The road follows the river; out of the shade and sunlight a wagtail darts and flies, a thin flash of pale yellow.

Grass snakes rustle in the withered leaves, their own carefree form of self protection.

As evening fell I bought a pheasant. At night I closed the window which looks out upon the river. I poured myself a drink. The water's sound grew distant through the window.

On the red lacquer of the dining table, I had let fall one pellet of shot.

Among the Branches

The dead of night, and over the thick dead leaves, a bear swings closer to the gingko tree, with one white candle lighted on its back. Its violent breath fills everywhere, and then is vanished in the forest's silence.

He watches this sleek furred mysterious beast, from way up among the branches. A solitary, Russian-looking man.

"Daddy, mummy's come back. Daddy, mummy's come back."

The voices of dead children are now birds. He hears them in the sky. His dead wife has now changed into a bear, and so she walks the forest.

But that can not be so; no, that's impossible. Thinking like that among the branches.

ANZAI FUYUE

Midwinter Writing
The Garden
Birthday
Birthday Again
Call
Sunflowers Are Already Black Gunpowder
Dice
Anniversary of the Marne
Estuary
The Thrush
Barren Fig Tree
The Path

Midwinter Writing

(Mes cahiers)

The evergreens are black; but my hands are always white. No evil sullies me.

The glittering axe.

Firewood chopped and scattered.

Work to be done even in midwinter.

And winter butterflies alight on straw, but you no longer make them out.

Wisteria-like waves soon gone to sleep; the animals we keep escape from winter now.

Only the road lies white before me, perhaps a hand pointing the way to go.

The Garden

Cherries

Cherries had tumbled down the mossed stone steps. The boy bit on the bitter taste of wisdom.

Souvenir

The spring moon lights a ghostly fan. Above the slippery stone steps. Skin beneath thin skin of ice. Bitter cherries from the tree; as wisdom fallen. The light scent here of moss. And then the splashing sound of the hot water.

Birthday

Under the flowering plum tree let me dream of far-off mornings.

The Mongolian officer I invited slips a doily secretly inside his breast coat pocket.

(Like a river disappearing in the desert.)

Now, Ammanese goldfish of mine,

Please look the other way,

Out of courtesy to our guest.

Birthday Again

I stuck a butterfly to the wall with a pin. It won't move any more. Happiness is like that.

The pet with its black ribbon on the dining table has the form a pet should have.

The water in the bottle is the bottle's shape.

And she in her chemise as her own beauty.

Call

My lacquered shoes are wafted into the sumptuous lobby of the H. Hotel, without once having to touch the ground. From the saloon of *The President McKinley*, in one swoop.

A deferential child appears, who just restrains himself from carrying me, and leads me to the finest suite.

Then for my sake he hangs up "Don't Disturb"; and then he says:

"A most unfortunate spring shower, sir."

"Ah yes, indeed. The pavements are quite wet."

Sunflowers Are Already Black Gunpowder

Grass seed floated in this evening's soup. One thousand islands.

The great majority of marksmen, for some unknown reason, have long, unkempt moustaches. On thinking about that it must provide "some form of resistance." (Smiles.)

Try writing "we" a number of times and it looks like children skipping. WeWeWeWeWeWeWe.

She (she being a domestic pet) has gentle creases in the corners of her eyes like Chekhov. Instead of a ribbon I shall give her a bone.

An autumn butterfly has settled on the towel I put inside the glass.

—Sunflowers are already black gunpowder.

Dice

    A spring moon lights up the western ocean on my globe. Above the oysters, that most skeptical of trades has grown a scant, blue beard. I am the Reuter special correspondent.

    Lisbon   my cuffs were soiled.

    Monte Carlo   crystal dice are smudged with finger prints.

    Abruptly   Peking.

    Tokyo   under thin ice the sweet witch is already moving.

Anniversary of the Marne

"Is that man Chinese?"

"Oh, don't be such a fool."

The brother and sister cling in pleasure to each other, and then they leave the room.

A plaintive music box at last begins its song from somewhere.

(Look, children, this is your own grandfather, who died in that terrible battle of the Marne. This is your brave, your marvelous grandfather.)

Estuary

A warped moon falls once more beyond the roofs and roofs.

The young girl was imprisoned there in that dry attic, tied up on the floor with harsh manila rope. Each night a Chinese would come, not even troubling to take off his shoes, and he would take her. While violated thus she dreamed a wide full flowing river there beyond those roofs, black consolation which allowed her fragile breast some small means of endurance.

And truly it flowed there, beyond those roofs and roofs after roofs, that broad full river flooding to the sea.

The Thrush

Heavy frost fell, shattering all the leaves on the cherry tree, and then departing. The black ribbon you had left behind was soiled with tears. Mari, I crossed the bridge again today, to buy that picture of the Baltic. Why? Still, it was gone; so that was that and I had nothing else to say; and so I went down town. I met Miss Winter there, laughing, doing an imitation of Mrs. Siddons. I alone seemed bored by it, and so she noticed how I looked and asked if there was something wrong.

How very, very cold. And indeed I said I did feel cold; but she just called me mad and condescended to rebuke me. I am an ignorant person so I could not fully grasp what she was saying.

Miss Winter said: "If I am wrong please do not hesitate to tell me so, because I am not all that clear about the things I say myself. You see I really like you. Of course, this really liking someone means so little anyway. Do you think that's strange of me?

"What do you think?"

What do I think? I think if it were possible that shattered leaves once more should go back to their branches. But this is something I can only ask myself. Surely there can be other springs for me like those I had. And as I tell myself so, far off somewhere a thrush begins to sing.

Barren Fig Tree

Under the fig tree I am flooded with a hatred of life, a feeling imprecise as the letter U.

At infants' school my disposition was considered awkward. With a duelling knife, because I had no one to duel with, I slashed something like boiling water into the cloudy bark of this dull tree.

Emotions; their object; her initial.

But she found it easier to give me up than even her text book of analytics.

I was not much good at technical subjects anyway.

Also I had this seemingly inborn dislike for our white uniform. I felt a frigid pathos for myself as something which gave shape to that pointless mass.

One cloudy afternoon, the result of having lost my sense of balance, I fell down from the Swedish bars.

My nervous foci had dislodged me.

And since that time the infection has gone on spreading, gradually rotting me away.

The Path

The first one to appear was the park keeper. He seemed to be one of those men who must be always muttering, always complaining or their health will suffer somehow. But this time we just passed him by. Which means that the requirements of velocity did not permit him any surplus energies, on this occasion, to be expended on his mutterings. Which seems to have soon had some effect upon his health. As proof of this when his libidinous eyes had fixed themselves in weird triangular fashion upon my heart and also on the place where Mari's must have been, he suddenly turned away from us and spat upon the opposite grass path. If he had not been ill he would surely hardly have spat in such a reckless fashion.

"He's sick."

"He's weird."

We then encountered a dog who seemed to be about his business. Having completed it he still discharged one more curious fragment as he passed us by. Certainly more of a romantic than the keeper. And last of all today's sea then appeared. The sea blew Mari's August clothes and passed.

"The sea. I feel an irritation when I think of it, the sea; an anger with no object. Yes, I mean anger, public indignation. I mean, even that keeper we just passed, I wouldn't say I have no sympathy with him at all. Do you think that's funny?"

"You're crazy."

And so we stretched out on the grass. While she was peeling fruit for me, I closed my eyes and I was falling.

Those soft, sweet sounds above finally opened a straight and narrow path within me. I thought of the park keeper, then the dog, the sea; of how this path within me must go on to other places. So opening my eyes.

    The sea was full of autumn.

TAMURA RYŪICHI

Etching
The Submerging Temple
The Golden Illusion
Autumn
Voice
Premonition
Images
Emperor
Winter Music

Etching

    This landscape seen once in a German etching   is now before his eyes   It is the aerial view of an ancient city as it goes from twilight into night   Or else it might be (this is thinkable) a modern sketch of some steep precipice as it is led from midnight toward dawn

    This man   the one whom I first spoke about murdered his father when he was quite young That autumn   his mother became beautifully insane

The Submerging Temple

    All men seek proof of death   yet no one who has witnessed it is here   So man himself is maybe an illusion   and so perhaps reality is no more than the greatest common factor of all things   In place of man objects themselves start questioning   they question about life   about their own existence   And even if this is all dreamed up in a chair yet it is something I must fear   And so reality perhaps is but the lowest common multiple of things   Still how can those who surely feel no sorrow at man's fate   how is it that they chance their bodies in this turbulent world   Geniuses have from time to time appeared   to give a more precise delineation of our nothing   self evident things that only give more depth to the revolving vortex of broad daylight

    Perhaps he was going to start telling us something But here I shall only write down the facts   He folded at the knees and then fell down   And men came running up   one of them a young man of about my age who whispered half unconsciously   "How beautiful his face is   The trouble is that it believes in the world   just in the way a flower does"

The Golden Illusion

He feared all ideas of the naked body   things of beauty must certainly destroy men   he had the habit of saying that

You don't see it with your eyes   you don't draw it with your hand   In broad daylight   in this city
    the autumn of 1947   I witnessed it   death's logical corroboration carved in golden script on a waxen breast

There was nothing to be sad about   but somehow he just stood there with moist eyes   and then said nothing but he looked   uncertainly in my direction

Autumn

    The bandaged rain turned as it fell   I wandered the sleepless city   in that autumn   and went to a small music concert   The concert room was closed in by parched doors   the callous pianist sits on a hard chair   and there from sleep the black forbidden dreams   distribute arms to all   Love   Love life with all your strength   you who can go armed now

    Beyond the door   rain smelling of fresh gauze turns again the corners of the streets   to the harbor   from the thin light of the harbor to the black dark sea   to an illusory world which has no stars

    My lips are wet   yet still my hands are parched Goodbye   woman who passes by me and goes out beyond the door   a tall man soaked in rain who waits for me   is it for life is it for death   the door between us as we load our guns

    Call blessings down   even for we solitary ones an enemy has appeared   in the mirror   my features are quite changed   a fiction of goose pimpled life Outside the door   the sleepless city and its satellite towns   from St. Petersburg in summer to a winter Paris   the woman   passionately sings   I love you still I love you still   and Tokyo autumn   The world is put together by my hands   dreaming under the antenna   this time a momentary awakening in sonata form   so everyone had better ask himself . . . and she says she desires   the freedom to choose death

    The applause has now begun   I rise up from my chair   mother

Voice

    Fingers start to hang over   this excavated ash-gray scale here

    Hold your breath   say as it is but voicelessly . . . Love is a twilit emblem   a discord of the genitals and the corpse   and she was beautiful on that day in the rain   and in the dawn that autumn   as she invites a golden smile I suddenly turn my back on her   blue fallen in the depth of eyes   For I have long been intimate with death   have witnessed all his obscene silences his holy dissolutions   experience being a form of witnessing   I have known the process which begins in screams and gradually changes to endearments   I have sometimes talked much with him from autumn into winter   when mist fills up the empty colored capital
    Deny all thought   for it is but the ownership of time   Break out from time to a heart rending space where the whole body feels   to feel   to feel our ideas with our bodies   Fingers start to hang over this excavated ash-gray scale here   the sounds are chosen by my fingers   and these sounds are pure matter which I sort out from all the putrefying kind cohesion comes   Is there something that I need to say now   twenty-five years   mother keeps calling for me in the passage and the garden   it turns to what seems an endearment   so let us never pray   that our youth should be one of fulfilment   weep   and if we weep then weep as father did   and if we weep it will not be for him

Premonition

   Afternoon comes unexpectedly   he is confined alone
in the depths of a chair   his hands hang down   and
the world clouds over   the sufferings of the world
assault him only   the sadness of the world digs out his
eyes   doors open like those wounds   he senses a way
back through there to the past

   Vaguely through the window he sees the town where he
was born   rain is falling on the town   these twenty
years   rain soaks the earth between one war and
another   some aspects of the town have changed
    also this town denies the town remembered of his
childhood   for then his mother had been beautiful
    his grandmother must have still been
on this earth   wordlessly the past comes through the
door and then joins up with one part of the future
and rain beats on against time   before his eyes the
rain is wounded   bandages for it then   obvious
middle aged men have raised too many obvious umbrellas

   What shall I do now   threatening hands come
through the open door and are laid on my shoulders
    cold lips are laid and lightly pressed on mine
a kiss which has no passion   yet I pathetically rejoice
in it

   I know that you have come to kill me

Images

a trickle of death,
this drab auburn town's
swarms of twisted entrails in the rain,
black umbrellas and their
flow of the knowledge of annihilation.

That man is not my father, nor is he my solitary friend. It is simply that we are the same existence, sharing the same experiences, the same images. Then, just as he, I was born during the first World War, and I most certainly died during the second.

Collapsing as a chair collapses. This is one of my oldest images, the eye in the swamp as desire for a death which is dreamed of.

With gouged-out eyes, cracked forehead, dull light in the hair, and then black garments soaked in a huge illusion of the sea and storm, when he appears, that shipwrecked man, with his screams, his savage chorus echoing, one night next week out of the mist which flows from autumn into winter, then I shall have to cry out also, asking where he has come from.

My tongue hangs out like a dog's.

Emperor

    In the stone there is an eye   an eye closed up in gloom and lassitude

    Black-suited he goes by my doorway   a winter emperor   my sad emperor   civilization's shadow on your chalk white forehead   as you walk on to Europe's graveyard   the sun full on your back   your self inflicted punishment is so pitiable

    Flowers!   you stretch out your hand   at this extreme end of the age of reason   at this limit of the age of progress   the world's winter now begins   the fair women of Europe are all shadows so who will set their lips upon your hand   parched brown by its drab fate does this palm of yours give any sign of burgeoning

    Flowers   scars like flowers

Winter Music

    You can't say that such things just cannot be   in some place unknown to me at the world's end   in what is certainly a basement room in some city deep in fog a thin twenty-five-year-old youth just like myself   blond hair   blue eyes   speaking in a northern European tongue   about the principles of revolutionary action
    madness or sentimentality perhaps   but who can now believe even if this were but the nausea of that winter of forty-seven   that this is still no concern of ours   Perhaps like a man in a Modigliani painting
    he leans his slender neck and looks straight at us
    and it's not certain what he's looking at   it is not clear   it is not certain   in a universe which too is now no longer clear   like a man who is at the point of waking up

    No one must laugh   even if it should be a fate more suited to the lowest kind of scum   no one must laugh
    Embrace this matchless destiny   kicking and protesting

    There is only you   probably the first and the last human being   I cast away all drama   involved in a much greater drama

    The singing voices go far off   the dangling hands the threatening footsteps fade away   from a basement room   from my desert   and where the city lights blink on and out   farewell to the sad formalities of time   farewell to the solemn days of usury

    Say this is all tied up with memories of childhood summer days   the smells when I'm alone on a night of snow   yet can not I imagine a way of life that has no

need of intellectual concepts   And so I studied from the pianist   and so I tried   with eyes and fingers to renew unceasingly a vision of this way of life   The wind begins to blow   So very well then   the universe is gradually turning cold   eye in the middle of a stone   Desperately praying for the fingers not to lose their poise   desperately praying for an eye much larger than my own   which must perhaps be called eternity   for those moments when the eye appeared
     And so he faintly smiles and questions me   gives the command for massacre of those concepts of the obvious the self-evident   in the space between the fingers and the eyes   in civilization's graveyard
     I stumble on into   winter music

YOSHIOKA MINORU

A Comedy
Confession
The Island
Legend
Winter Painting
Simple
Solidity
Recuperation
The Lovely Journey

A Comedy

    In a corner of the kitchen   an egg with its back peeled off pops up   Near the banks of the long night   a man who was sleeping there has risen
   With a cat wearing a cap perched on his shoulder   he digs a hole for his wife who will die   A handcart loaded with food and gold goes out the other way   the proper road being blocked by the legs of the bed and various utensils   Because the weeping man is stroking it
   the mouse in the cat's throat dissolves in botryoidal form   His tears put out the moon before him   finally cover with snow the wood   where trees from far off had changed their direction   and call back the man and the slant-eyed cat to his small room   although there's no question of walking   He had always enjoyed his glass before the fire   Because the cat was running about in the attic   this man who feels the cold desired a molted cat   but closes his eyes bedazzled by such total nakedness   The birds which look that night in through the window   all take the shape of the hair of his dead wife and so he shoots them down   He patiently untangles the cat's four legs   and what his wave of a hand sinks into is a dish of over-yellow butter
   Attracted by such dangerous culture   this man with a doctor's beard sweats over it   but the cat accidentally breaks the glass   and it was that which certainly must have saved the man then   A finger in the vaporizer stops the acceleration of amoeba   and since these have degenerated into human hands   bright from the fragments blood flowed out as well   maybe because they had felt like bearing something heavy   So the man looks about him   astonished to find he is enclosed by scissors and hard household furniture   So of those parts which are

not to be wounded   legs face genitals he quickly takes great care   From out of a strong leather bag   he does not reappear twice

Confession

    What I don't know   I don't tell other people   Also I don't walk about the plaster formed by other people's voices   I just gather up all my strength   and try like mad to make this tiny axe touch something   If it's something standing up   I push it down on a stone until it breaks   If it's something lying down I jump on it
    If it's something that revolves I wind it round my hand   until it bites right into my black flesh   then make way for the rows of ants and the blood vessels which mournfully come out   And if it's a woman I push it back in her eyes   I shall wait patiently until I brim quite full with adequate grace and cold lake water   If it's food I spit it out   into the darkness under the table where the bottles and utensils have sunk down   While cutting off one by one the heads of birds and fish   I classify the useful and the useless   although there's always the chance of making a mistake here   And when I do I wipe up all the feathers and bubbles of fish scale   and have a look at what is going on outside the window   seeing the children skipping   the mass of chimneys giving birth to a whole night   Finally with a scream like that which sleeps right down the grain of trees   I start off running   in the shape of a naked man   then a black elephant embodiment of all that dedicated training   I go on soaked in the rain   At this point I have something I can tell to other people

The Island

    Landing on the island   the man discovers in the corners of the rocks   various large curved fragments of the bones of animals and fish   the rotating sun has blackened   contraction of a black octopus head   The man's eye gradually drops to the horizon   a margin where an angular moon rises   Try to forget   Now with extreme lucidity   a sea bird's egg approaches
    Why can one never hear music at such moments   It is the time when sleepless arcs are given shape   The man lies stretched out and his distant hands and feet move slightly   at which time from its lower edge
    the area of the island starts contracting   This must be the nest of tomorrow's setting sun   For the sake of illusory birds which never will take flight   the egg is magnified at the man's side   On its whole surface savagely bleached in the light   one can find nowhere marks of the fingernails of adventurous people
    He does not choose   this Atlas   From the thin womb this man wrings out a little voice and blood   Insulated from him on the other side   the winter waves continue to glide by

Legend

    Jumps down   from the chair   a naked leg covered in cat's fur   All over in a moment but   in close-up   it is swallowed up into the folds of a flower   Anyone would be surprised at this the first time   for the four wooden legs   lumber across the floor a while
    then suddenly come to a halt in a corner of the room
    and the chair is transformed into legend   Unaware of this event a man   appears out of the blanket he'd been wearing round his head   and sits down on the chair   While extracting the circulating heat and stench   he earnestly pays out the tube linked up to his anus   in the form of an uncontrollable rubber hose
    which then becomes so bulky   it wriggles about and fills up all the room   Things palpitating
    Pleasure's elasticity   For the sake of the night   this man has for a very long time now   his face beside the cat's   surrounded as he is on all sides by the tube been holding in his breath   At the moment when he disappears   he screams out there's a fire

Winter Painting

   Other people can't see these things but   there are a number of them in my room   For example between the legs of the bed and the wall   are placed the boots which I took off a week ago   One is fallen and folded over   the other is just standing up   soaked only in the rain of my clandestine memories   they dry beneath my bed of evil habits   and they split   My landlady visits my room for just one reason   when the cat is going to have kittens   it drags its thick hairy brush of a tail about the floor   and so from morn to night the landlady plies her broom   I become quite ill   behaving like a lobster under the blankets   My landlady being a shore-dweller   wearing slippers   does not perceive in the shadow of the rocks   in the swaying of the seaweed   the opening closing symptoms of this person   moistened by the sea   She puts the new-born kittens in a cardboard box and she goes out   I open the bay window slightly on the night   This is the most important part of the day's routine   My landlady takes off her clothes   restores the body warmth and suppleness of the six kittens sunken in the river   Hot water overflows the bath   and I'm in danger now   Halfway up a staircase with a top and a bottom   I discover   leaning against a wall   a canvas by a painter who committed suicide   Among all my possessions   only that one can endure the light   Perhaps that only can protect me   from the rose-colored earthquake in my landlady's thighs   The impoverished painter drew to his heart's desire   this angry composition   where from a deep hollow   near or far   exhausted torsos made of stone   are struggling to get out

Simple

    The man died without being given any warning   His wife felt only hatred for   this man whose coccyx so prominently projected   His tongue shone coldly in the region of his eyes and so   this was intolerable to his voluminously breasted wife   Except at meal times   his movements were extremely sluggish   so one could say in fact that he made none   Especially when he went to bed   he made her feel that part which has no flower attached   and dragged along by a spider's thread   the man would bend to the ground in a most wretched posture   However his dead wife couldn't have cared less about all that   Just each day unfailingly with rippling hand   feeding the dog kept on the other side of the wall   Such perjury he believed sincerely would not kill her   A cat which had inherited his good qualities   was covered in snow up on the roof its very being alive being vexatious   Suppose one's own snake belly were to sufficiently extend   from out of the inner darkness   thrust back into the room where the man wanders   then one might stand some kind of chance   Because a plaster embryo had been conceived   the dog would obtrude its services on the man annoying him making him laugh so   that the former delicious operation would become impossible
    Then the man in order to stay alive   would call down his dead wife's cat from the roof where it only raised the dust   and then consider teaching it some tricks   none of your vulgar popular affairs   but turn it into a beautiful woman   warming it in the bed on the bridal night   and make it climb the moon loved by the drowned   A huge cry then let forth enough to make known   the half-ripe shame of the peach which holds its breath beneath the leaf and the shape of naked woman   Summer came dangling strings of lightning

Did the man die as proof that he was human His head exciting the dog's blood the lower half of his body covered in cat's fur he was buried out of this country of sweat in a small shivering mountain village

Solidity

    My prejudices trouble a good many people   if ever I apply a razor blade to a stalk which is the stalk of a plant   I discover that tragic rose-colored unraisable family deploying from the wound thereof   This thin-membraned couple   not drinking water   not being able to smile at light   in the rustling of their intercourse   stain the walls and the bedclothes with pollen
    which when you touch it feels much like a rough powder   For which reason their children do not run about in any world of toy cars   their playground being their mother's womb   So I slip under   the rows of gourds all in the shade there   and briskly leave this pastoral   since my belief is   that things should be quite hard and pleasant to the touch   The propped up axe menaces both me   and the dragonfly's compound eyes   So I exhaustively transfer myself to   a total track suited posture   bearing on my back an incomparable rainbow and an ice pick for the mountains   I dislike all types of squashy frogs   Something like hard wings   hard rain I fondle with both hands   Just as a try-out I take a kick at a can   and in a way people could hardly credit   I enter the town in ecstasy   I knock on the outer stone wall of a besieged temple
    This indeed is royal sport   pursuing a pregnant girl on her way to the hospital   As one goes further up the rise   the striped mesh of the stones turns to the center drawing one thin line   and at the unbearably slippery summit   shows a white stomach   This is the moment when the doctor laughs   an evening of fires the bells all clanging wildly   The forceps and the moving scissors stretch out taut the skin   going to greet the head in the middle of the bag   The surrounding dandelion seeds   are painfully damaged and plucked off   Fat splatters over the spotless track

suit   I then see real solidity and so become all
flustered   overlooking the coarse irresponsible armies
of blood advancing along the fragile tracts of the body
beneath   At which point I quit the town   The wind
transforms me to a frozen man   a sliding object
and that's the reason why I usually don't smile   don't
even say goodbye

Recuperation

    Munching a pickled onion   that's my way of spending a pleasant time   Tucked in the deep folds of the ward blankets   I wait with great fortitude   not to be cured and also not for death   but for the light of the wearing away of things   It is now April   and the thighs of the bees tremble   over the fields and the skin piling up with pollen   the moon of the end of fleshly desire approaches   My fractured thigh bone from its long repose   hears the music of the blood   becoming phosphorescent   or it generates vitality   as a black walking stick   showing the rusty fade out of a pastoral landscape   Remaining stuffed like that in a mountain of straw   without raising copulative cries   it sets two crows off flying   Sometimes my sister comes to visit me   extolling the malignantly affected parts of the neighboring patients   Her pummelling of my lowered head   entices for a moment the pomegranate's explosion   I usually take my walk in the frozen garden   attracting rather than flocks of cranes or nurses   the advances of a hideous woman   Whipping up a womb of sexy dreams and prosaic dictionaries   I then sniff a powerful medicinal smell   and am suddenly smeared in the balm of resurrection   a gradual death assaults me   The established concepts of death are stolen away   In the form of a camel   which since her childhood the woman had considered a loathsome beast   I kneel down   Troubles occur in any world   On the stretcher carried out   this is a daybreak   where the friction between starched flesh and bones begins   Thirst mediates with the eyes   overflows from the swamp where the ice had started melting   My tail soaked like a viviparous fish   I drink the water up all in one gulp

The Lovely Journey

    The antique steward clears away and goes   not so much going outside the door as being sucked into the sunset's sphere   His liveried trousers leave a blue stain   in a corner of the sparkling floor of the cabin   where a couple are like tapeworms on the bed
    The antique steward will die no doubt   whelmed in these waves of threatening napkins   in this violent rolling   And then set out for distant lands of beautiful stones   astride a spoon of peeling plate   all kinds of rotting meat and vegetables   With the elegant deportment of firm wrapping   the antique steward flies up to a crudely carved out sky   Goodbye   you crowds of cudgels   everydayness of bags   the sea of boxes   From way up here things are easy to work out   the melodrama of conflagrations   the end of the lonely ceremony of thunderstorms   The antique steward takes the warm meal away with practiced hand   After all that who would complain that his midday nap was a trifle long   Who can be truly acquainted with the habits of the dead   With the effort of getting up the antique steward's gilt buttons all fly off   and he seeks them on that rolling surface   With an enormous splash as he strikes the water   the antique steward has made the first real blunder in his life
    Now facing the huge numbers of dead passengers in the seaweed's shade   he tenders his most profound apologies   for in order to see the long dream which follows this   one must endure bewilderment and shame   As one of the successful he grows fat   and enters a secret grotto   For a while his eyes are dazzled by the beautiful gold haired girls there   The moon rolls under a wine cask   This may well turn out to be a most improper graveyard

YOSHIOKA'S "THE ISLAND": AN INTERPRETATION

Yoshioka Minoru's poems are no less difficult to read in the original than in these English versions, so the necessity of providing glosses on them is debatable. Consequently this one has been set here, after the reading of the poems. However, the reader might find some indication of how the poem could be read useful, since his other poems invite similar readings. The reader of Japanese is referred to the analysis by Professor Shinoda Hajime in *Gendaishishū* (see Bibliographical Note p. 57), which I have made use of here.

The poem is no attempt to recreate the actual stuff of experience, but has the same relationship to lived reality as does a Picasso painting. The poem is, in fact, held together by its geometrical shapes, although bits of a very naked reality keep intruding. Perhaps what gives his poems their peculiar life is the way in which an apparently abstracted and fantastic world always gives the impression of speaking about personal realities. Of the poems translated here only the final one, "The Lovely Journey," appears not to do so, having consequently a lightness of tone close to the more orthodox modernism of Anzai Fuyue.

> Landing on the island   the man discovers in the corners of the rocks   various large curved fragments of the bones of animals and fish   the rotating sun has blackened   contraction of a black octopus head

This opening sounds as though it might be about a real island with allegorical overtones, but this impression is soon canceled out by that final phrase. The real poem can be said to start from "contraction of a black octopus head," for that phrase refers backward and forward in a way which upsets the almost rational movement of the beginning, leading to the following anti-logical sequence:

> The man's eye gradually drops to the horizon   a

>   margin where an angular moon rises   Try to forget
>   Now with extreme lucidity   a sea bird's egg
>   approaches

In the grammar of the original the phrase, "contraction of a black octopus head," stands isolated as it does in the translation, and whether one should read it as an image of the sun, or as something independent that the sun illuminates, or as an image of the man's eye, is an open question, since the poem insures that the question remain open. A sequence of images is created, but none of them has interpretative power over the others. What we have is a circular shape that turns, and contracts into various images. We then see that the island is related to this, a circle cut off from what surrounds it. One of these circles, the man's eye, is then halted in its movement by the straight line of the horizon (that limit to human curiosity, as Baudelaire called it), from which an angular moon (the moon as a flawed, incomplete circle) rises. This then attains the fullness it always implies, and becomes a bird's egg (the ideograms for island and bird are very similar ones, and there is an overlapping of images here which the translation can not show).

>   Why can one never hear music at such moments   It is the time when sleepless arcs are given shape   The man lays stretched out and his distant hands and feet move slightly   at which time from its lower edge   the area of the island starts contracting   This must be the nest of tomorrow's setting sun   For the sake of illusory birds which never will take flight   the egg is magnified at the man's side   On its whole surface savagely bleached in the light   one can find nowhere marks of the fingernails of adventurous people

The poem now becomes a study of man's relationship to time, the element in which he lives, and of his efforts to comprehend and escape from it. In the imagistic world of the cinema it is music which gives meaning to actions

(Sartre envied the screen hero because his most trivial action was performed to music, and thus he was redeemed from the contingency which haunts our everyday lives). The man dreams his meanings and these sleepless arcs (sun, moon, island of the self) are given shape; yet the dreaming man, since he exists and moves, can not give total meaning to his own being since he is himself a part of it. Thus his island contracts, not filling the whole of being, and he thinks again in terms of time, of this moon, this egg being in time, the cause of tomorrow's sun. This round nest is for illusory birds which will never take flight, the egg, or moon, becoming the sign of human endeavor, for the moon looks soiled because of its markings, and our thoughts have indeed handled it. But these mental adventures have left no real marks on it (the poem was written well before the moon landing).

    He does not choose   this Atlas   From the thin womb this man wrings out a little voice and blood   Insulated from him on the other side   the winter waves continue to glide by

All these pure shapes mean solitude, isolation (insulation) from the wintry sea as it continues to glide by. From this isolation the poet wrings out a small amount of blood, his voice, his words. Thus he has created these shapes, a certain life, from the images of death with which the poem begins.

I do not wish to claim any authoritative status for this interpretation, since the poem is not of the kind which permits one to speak with authority about it. Other emphases might well be possible, and any reader might read it in different ways at different times. However, the way the poem works has perhaps been shown by this, and his other poems should be read in much the same way.

TANIKAWA SHUNTARŌ

The Sanctity of Trivial Things
Scissors
Inaccessibility of the Glass
Pleasure and Pain of Looking at a Glass
Persistency of Apple
Conditions of Growth
A Personal View of Gray
Watching her Play in Water
Details for the End of the World
Pseudo-anatomical Self-portrait
A Proper Sentence for the Open Window

The Sanctity of Trivial Things

Trivial things which vaguely lie in trivial forms and ways connected in no way to other things of no account. How to account then for their trivial being in the world, when there's no way of finding out that can be found? Trivia lying idly in indifferent poses pose no threat to our own being the time being, although the no-accountedness of things of no account accounts perhaps for our continuing confusions over them.

These things can unaccountably brush hairily against our hands, or flash and dazzle to confront our eyes. They make a noise that deafens sometimes, or they can shock the tongue with bitterness. And so distinguishing trivia from one another is to forgo definitively that in which true triviality lies. And so to grasp the trivial in one exclusive yet illimitable shape would not then contradict with seizing trivia as these countless finicky bits of no account, and yet such triv . . . (this part has been blotted out).

The writer cannot speak of trivial things in trivial ways. He speaks of things of no account as if indeed they always were of some. And so to measure them, to argue for their use or uselessness, to stress the fact that they are there, accounting for the feel and taste of them, is only to breed more illusions over things of no importance. The reason that they are beyond our definition lies maybe in the structure of our language, or in the fact of language wrought as style, or simply in perhaps some intellectual failing of the author? The reader is free to judge this as he will.

Scissors

Now they are on the desk and my eyes see them. Now I can pick them up. Now I can cut out the shape of a man in paper with them. Now perhaps I can cut off all my hair with them. Of course I am not considering the possibility of using them to murder someone with.

And yet, however, they grow rusty, will gradually grow blunt, grow old and worn. They might retain their usefulness, but in fact they will be finally thrown away. There's no way now of knowing if they were made of Chilean iron, or touched by Kruppsian fingers; and yet the fact that something of that kind had once been so means they escape the form men gave them; and it's not difficult to guess at some quite formless destiny to which they might return. And now upon the desk they tell us of the time when that will be; although they coldly tell all this to no one in no words, behaving as if they were not behaving so. Men made these things to be of use to them, but far beyond such usefulness they unavoidably exist as they do now. There is no need to call them scissors. They have already countless other names. The fact that I don't use their other names is not just a mere custom I conform to, but more no doubt a form of self-defense.

The reason things like this have power to pull words out of me, untangling the threads and threads of words within me, is that the danger they might turn to yet more rarefied existences than they are now, always lies open here.

Inaccessibility of the Glass

In most cases it's a cylinder with a bottom but no top. An upright cavity. Limited space closed in upon its own gravitational center. It is maintained within the earth's magnetic field, so it does not allow a fixed amount of water to disperse. When it is only filled with air we call it empty, and then its shape is lucidly shown by light, and we can gauge the substance that it is, not by the use of measuring devices, but by one cold, confirming glance.

Flip it with the finger, it vibrates and makes a noise. This can be used sometimes as a signal, or very rarely as a note in music; although this high reverberation has a kind of rigid self-importantness about it which overrides such uses and offends the ear. It is placed on the dining table. Or it is held in someone's hand. Sometimes it slips from that hand and falls. Indeed, because it has this tendency, is capable of being smashed, transforming into fragments of itself, it thus conceals lethal potentialities.

Yet even after being smashed it does not cease existing. Should every single one on earth be smashed to powder in an instant, still we could not be rid of them. They have been named: in various culture systems by differing signs perhaps, but they would still exist then for each one of us as an unaltering concept, and should the making of them (of glass, or even of wood or iron or clay) be totally forbidden by the most severe of laws, we still would not be free from nightmares that contained them.

Tools mainly used to quench our thirst, and though they serve no better function than our hollowed palms both cupped together if ever that extreme need should arise, yet in the various complexities of our lives, in slant rays of the morning sun, or in an artificial light, they have an undeniable and silent beauty.

Our skill, experience, our intelligence have brought these forth; and we have named them, have bestowed on them this very natural sounding syllable. Yet is this right for them? For it's not sure that anyone knows for certain.

Pleasure and Pain of Looking at a Glass

There is a glass upon the wooden table, with water in it. Light from a sixty-candle-power lamp shines on it from the left, casting a rainbow-colored specter of extreme faintness on the side of this cylindrical glass object, but giving no adornment to the water there inside.

This glass has not been filled with water to quench someone's thirst; more likely this has been the aimless act of someone in the family (a child perhaps); or it's been set there as a kind of game; and though it looks quite ordinary, still it creates a tension in the observer. This tension is not brought about by that fragility contained within its very quality as glass, nor by the possibilities of altered contents which plain water can suggest, but on the contrary comes much more from a sense of its unchanging immobility. Just stretching out the hand could instantaneously destroy the glass, the water in it (and the soft shadow there upon the table), but nothing can be done about the fact that it exists as it does now.

Although its immobility has nothing in it of eternity, yet it stands like a riddle before all. So it escapes all our attempts to shape it or express it with our words, is not to be portrayed in painting or in sculpture. Because of this it lacks not only any ambiguity, but takes on more and more of clarity; a plenitude of clarity which draws the observer near and nearer to the concept of the poem.

And that is right, you see, for all that I can see there is the poem now. Bright fullness of the light, the wordless poem which no hands approach, which fills me, all fretfulness and striving gone away, as I attain a peace which seems a form of drunkenness.

Persistency of Apple

It can't be red; it is no color, it is apple. It can't be round; it is no shape, for it is apple. It can't be sour; it is no taste, for it is apple. It can't cost much; it is no price, for it is apple. It can't be nice; it is no beauty, it is apple. It can't be classified; it is no plant, for it is apple.

Flowering apple; fruit-bearing tree swaying its branches in the wind. Apple beaten by rain, and pecked at by the birds; apple torn down. Apple wind-fallen to the ground. Apple which will rot, and which is seed and sends forth shoots. Apple which does not have to be called an apple. Apple which does not need to be an apple, and which does not mind being an apple either; apple which in itself contains all other apples, whether itself is apple or is not.

All kinds of apples: Royal Reds and Country Brights, Imperial Bells and Jubilees, and Empresses and Crimson Harbingers; in ones and threes and fives and dozens, or twenty pounds of them or twelve or two million tons. Apples cultivated and transported. Weighed, wrapped, transacted apples. Disinfected apples which will be digested, distributed, disappear. Apples! Apples?

Yes, that is apple, that thing there, there, that there. That over there, that in the basket. That falling off the table, transferred to the canvas, that baked in an oven. The one a child will take into his hand and bite, that one. No matter how many may be devoured or rot, still they swarm right back up on the branches, then endlessly appear to glitter in the shops. What are these all a replica of? When was it made?

Apple which can make no reply. Apple which can not question either. Apple which can tell us nothing, being apple only and all apple still. . . .

Conditions for Growth

To rise up softly, to achieve a single shallow depth, then spread out slantwise, to contort, to sharply twist and bend, enfold in many folds. . . .

Sometimes to waver, swell unceasingly (the whole shape as a flowing), and at the same time to climb up and up, with moments of still equipoise but swaying gently to the following moment, at last in quiet sinuousness to glide —

To open up unknown then, shrink at times, to link both front and back together, smoothly reversing (spasmodically contracting), swelling out again, and springing, dragging, hardening, dissolving; then filling out again, then drowsily stagnating, then convulsing.

Crinkling and rustling and yet staying absolutely silent —

Power arrives from elsewhere, it gives birth to power here, quarrels with other forms of power, squirms as if caught in a net of power, and will spread endlessly by its own power, in its eternally unending lack of system, with a discursive rhythm which can not be grasped.

(It seems to be returning whence it came, but never losing its direction.)

This is no close-up nor any bird's-eye view. Cradled among the stars this flesh-made cradle where we dwell and grow, fortunate in our endless trance.

A Personal View of Gray

No matter how white a white may be, there is no instance of the truly white. In flawless white there is the faintest blackness hidden unseen to the eye, the always actual structure of the white. White is no enemy of black, but rather white as whiteness gives birth to the black, which should be thought of more as something that it fosters. The very moment when white has its being it has begun to give birth to a blackness.

And yet, in its long journey into blackness, white stays quite resolutely white, no matter how much euphony with gray it may proceed through, until the moment it achieves real black. Although it may be sullied by those things which cannot be thought of as its attributes, by shadowing, by dullness, by absorption of the light, still white shines out beneath the shadow of gray's mask. White dies in one swift moment, in vanishing with no trace of whiteness, as the true blackness then appears. And so —

No matter how black black may be, there is no instance of the truly black. In lifeless black there is the faintest whiteness like a gene hid unseen to the eye, the always actual structure of the black. The very moment when black has its being it has begun to give birth to a whiteness. . . .

Watching Her Play in Water

First of all the footmarks wet from water vanished, and then the charming dimples and round eyes. The pink nails vanished, the black curls; and at that moment when the knees vanished the blue sky went as well; as did the flowers, and all the letters vanished quite soon after. Of course the soldiers vanished too, and all the tools, the saws, the hammers, pliers; and one could well conclude that all ideas had vanished in the same way also. Everything disappeared, from the most certain to the least precise of things.

In such a situation to say that "all had disappeared" is but the worn out cliché of the idle poet, because the "all had disappeared" had disappeared as well, as also the "all had disappeared had disappeared as well" had disappeared; and yet before there had been time to grow infatuated with this verbal game, the next moment a wriggling trout appeared. And as one took that in back came the stream, then a briefcase whose owner was unknown, the legal dictionary, and then two-thirteen in the afternoon; and elsewhere lovers started to appear again. Then in the twinkling of an eye the footmarks wet with water came back too, and then the little girl (five years five months), with her stark-naked belly with its bare button in the center of it; and then her wonderfully contented smile again appeared.

Details for the End of the World

Although there is no wind green apples will fall from the branches. The sheep let loose will start to bleat, and even when night falls they will not cease. Creaking doors will become light as feathers, and book marks fall from out the pages; and then quite suddenly, in the newly opened Opera House, the singer's voice will fail to reach the circle. That cracks should open in stained glass is unavoidable perhaps, but that the children will no longer cry is something much more difficult to bear. The ants will go back to their nests no more but wander lost among the blades of grass; and when all chiming clocks begin to sound a half note higher, then socks will fall down each time they're pulled up, the table legs go numb, and wallpaper will break out in a rash. Jealous feelings will not disappear, however, but grow much more and grow more violent; because the heads of households can do nothing positive about this, their bellies will turn hard and flat as boards, then cave in like the bottom of a ship.

Coffee beans will reveal the warehouse floor, and when the sideways looking knave begins to stare full face, then camels from the zoo will start to lumber in the streets. Like cripples the stars will edge close to each other, iron sculptures be recast as enormous mallets, the Buddhas on the mandalas gird up their loins and go back up the stream, the pregnant women form processions for no reason; and all that happens will be premonitions of what is to come; yet medals will still go on being received, although the details of the world will gradually start to lose their rough irregularity, and their peculiar stench.

Spirals will cease spiraling, straight lines will lose their tension and will sag; while circles twist, and parallels turn their backs upon each other as they drift away. When smiles at these absurdities appear the muscles will no longer be attached to skin. What seem to be tin fragments will go on falling from the sky without end. In the idiot's face there will reside the signs of wisdom which the human race has so far not been able to attain. The atmosphere will all be sucked into a vacuum. All languages on earth, those written and unwritten, will be gathered up into an O-shaped scream; and when silence gently whirls to hold that scream in its embrace, then one lone dandelion seed will fail to make its way to earth, and idly float about my face.

Pseudo-anatomical Self-portrait

I ate some strawberries. I have molar teeth filled up with gold. I saw the young leaves of a tree whose name I do not know. I have an iris in each eye. I drove a nail into some plywood. I have biceps in my upper arms. I kept repeating a phrase of a half remembered song. I have a sublingual mound. In the air of the street I smelled the scent of the makeup of a girl as she went by. I have a glans penis. I referred to the dictionary a number of times while I wrote down words. I have phalangeal bones. When I fail to understand what really matters, I can still keep on writing. I have temporal lobes.

I am forbidden to know precisely what I am. Yet I have phenyl pyruvic acid in me. I keep discovering that I secretly enjoy the misfortunes of my friends; and what sustains the structure that I am which feels like that is, among other things, the sacroiliac I have. Since I possess tactile neurons I can perceive the sweating skin of the drunkard who accosts me on the train, but I have no wish to recognize that he has the same neuroglia as myself.

I suppose I shall not be able to avoid being my own captive till I die. I sense a slight vertigo at the thought. I have cochlear canals which via the earth's gravity make contact with interstellar matter. I shall be burned sometime in the incinerator. Leaving behind just one unciform cartilage.

A Proper Sentence for the Open Window

The window has been opened. The open window is connected with the landscape by a twisted rope of wind. No, because it happens that my gaze determines through the open window how the focus of the external world will change, so only a minor fraction of that world can be observed. No, the open window has been decorated with a fading, ocherous paint. No, the open window transmits faint sounds from the outside to the inside of the room, by way of the air which circulates and fills its open portion. No, the open window, through the fact of being open, records the action of the man who opened it some minutes past. No, the open window modestly displays, as it has done for half a century now, the various skills of men who made it.

No, the open window is a minimal illusion. Description of the various details of it mainly serve as a cheap material whereby the speaker may console himself with words. No, the open window is a useless concept which gives birth to a transient sense of solidarity between one person and some others. No, the open window in this moment now is a symbolic generalization of all the immeasurable windows in the world. No, the open window is one of those images which are perpetually degraded from existential status into metaphor. No, the open window can not be destroyed in even the most willfully fantastic literary contexts. No, the open window is quite meaningless. No, the open window lets in hatred.

An ant crawls on the window frame. The window has been opened.

INOUE YASUSHI

In the Mountains
Weasel Slash
A Life
The Eye
Love
A Departure
June
The Olive Forest
The Arctic Ocean
Dawning
The River Indus
The Boy
River Light
The Beginning of Autumn
The Kite
Green Leaves
Youth
One Month, One Day
Elegy
The Pool
The Ancient Capital
Old Man in a Turban
The Evening Sun
A Light Rain in Autumn
Travel

In the Mountains

Osaka; two o'clock at night; a newspaper editor's office underground; that time of chronic idleness and boredom, after the air raid warning's sound, and listening for the dull and heavy drone of the B29s, which five minutes later would methodically fill up the sky. And then I thought of that small mountain village far inland, where I had sent my wife and children off to safety just three days before.

It was a plateau; not the sense of mountains, but a feeling more of being near the sky. The wind blew always from the northwest there, and all around bloomed wild blue flowers whose name I did not know.

Indifferent to all time's changes, in that one corner of the mountains, year after year, the quiet white summer clouds would rise; and silently each snow deep night would turn into the next and pass.

And thinking so I fell into a sudden, deep emptiness; no sense of comfort, consolation, nor even one of my own solitude. More like the sadness in the eyes of some living creature which has hidden its mate in a hole up on the hill. There in the depths of those dark velvet eyes it drifts: something we call the bitterness of life.

Weasel Slash

On the way to school we passed over a steep gully, the scene of a battle long ago. At noon it was deep in the gloomy shade of trees, and, looking from the bridge, you saw at the bottom there always the same small patches of still water, with damp, fallen leaves. They said the monster weasels came out as the sun went down, so all of us were frightened of the place.

I never once in fact saw one of those weasels, nor ever heard the tread of one of them. That was because these things came up like the wind, and then with one quick stroke of their keen sickles would slash the faces or the thighs of people. When we were kept on late at school working for our exams, then it was sheer terror to pass that place. We folded our satchels tight under our arms, and raced across the bridge.

One day at school a young teacher gave us the scientific reason for this weasel slash. A local vacuum forms in the atmosphere, and this sudden fall of pressure down to zero affects the human body like sharp razor blades. Our gully satisfied all that was required to bring about this atmospheric phenomenon.

From then on my fear of these disquieting monsters vanished from me. But the first step my mind took to despair at human life probably happened at the same time too. Often I call to mind those monster weasels still. Suddenly, quite suddenly, midway contingencies in all men's fate, the severing blow of the weasel slash is given, by these chance pockets of such frigid air.

That gully was buried under long ago. For some years now a red dirt road has led straight on to what was an imperial army airfield.

A Life

"When I was young I'd go without food and sleep thinking of ways to get an enormous yellow chrysanthemum up into the night sky. Sometimes I even used to jump from bed, dreaming I'd seen that bright yellow flower pop open, then fade away into the pitch black dark. Still, the fact remains I never could get any yellow out of fireworks.

So the old pyrotechnist briefly said, laying hands stained with gunpowder on his knees, lowering his speckled face.

He never managed to create his yellow chrysanthemum, but in his time he had no equal for the speed at which he worked. Sixty set off in just one minute; and the way he hurled ball after exploding ball into the tube whose baseplate burned white-hot; that was a skill which was surely close to genius.

And always then he would squarely turn his back upon this festival of burning arrows, those hundreds he had launched into the sky, obstinately turning his thin frame of sixty solitary years away, deliberately vanishing in the nitrous smoke.

The Eye

It must have been when I was seven years old. It was a bright spring day with a strong wind blowing, and somebody was carrying me on his back, and I peered down into the old well that was there in a corner of the garden. Mossed-over layers of stone with thick ferns growing; a coldness in the air which made you shiver; and at the bottom of that square tube fallen so far from the surface of the earth, unmoving water placed like a rusty mirror. It seems now that it was then that something quite decisive in my life crept for the very first time within my body.

If I had not had that moment in my childhood, if I had not seen the assassin's frigid eye buried in some dark place within the earth. . . . Then maybe at twenty I could have slashed a friend between the eyes; at twenty-five gone wild over some political cause; at thirty staked my life on the love of a woman; at thirty-five despaired and crossed that Chinese river; or at forty made some kind of name for myself.

But everything turned out quite differently; and by the wild waters of that river in North China, in a glittering sunlight which is not of this world, I knew the intoxication of fierce conflict which cares nothing about death. And since that time I have been indolent; only a looker-on at life.

Love

Joining in the prattle of my five-year-old child, I felt a sudden motioning in the blood, seized by a love I had no way of resisting. I understood that I must bear this burden, suffer the violent love I had for the child, perhaps until I died. And thinking so I found myself in a deep valley of desolation. And all day long that day I felt my back washed by a white wind unceasingly.

Mingling with the crowds in the bright-lit places; or in the luxurious study of a friend, turning the pages of new photos of the Himalayan expedition; nothing I did could mend the way I felt.

Up until evening; in the cold wind of the sea standing alone on the bank at the river mouth, watching the countless white-flecked waves break in toward me; all day that day something was taking a savage revenge on me.

A Departure

As if a bouquet of flowers had been thrown among us the carriage's closed-in evening gloom turned suddenly light. The train had stopped at a small fishing village at the very tip of the peninsula, and then these three, two sisters and a brother, boarded it there. The eldest girl must have been near twenty, her sister fifteen or sixteen, and finally the brother was around twelve or so. They relayed in their seven pieces of luggage, put them up on the compartment rack, then opened the window (the train was already moving), and all three poked their faces out, calling after their mother waving their hands. There was a bank with the white wall of some expensive-looking house, and a white figure stood there in the dark; mother, no doubt, because she raised her hand and waved back to them.

At last they closed the window, then sat down and giggled at each other. And so the elder girl relaxed with a paperback, the young one lowered her lovely, sorrowful, anxious face, and the boy brought out an apple which he then began to polish on his trousers.

Twenty years later I wondered what days they had spent, those three then in the flower of their youth. And I shuddered in unlucky premonition. And so I truly prayed for them; I offered prayers of such a fervency as I had never done for those close to me; prayed for the happiness of those who had then seemed to carry light and gaiety about them. Because that night I could conceive no new departures for them, save only those traveling toward fresh grief.

June

The blue of the sea grows faint; to that degree the blue of the sky grows deeper.

People wear blue suits in the streets, and so with that blue vanishes from the fields and mountains.

June: coming and going of all blueness. To bypass these back-and-forth proceedings, I myself must set out on a journey.

The Olive Forest

The hundred miles from Cordova to Seville are buried under wave after wave of hills, those hills themselves buried in olive trees. Olives as far as the eye can see. During midday the leaves turn up, showing their glittering, silver undersides; but as the sun goes down they change back to one mass of angry, silent, dull dark green. One straight paved road, complying to the will of something, drives unrelentingly across this olive region.

When I arrived in the old town of Seville at eight o'clock that night, I was totally exhausted. The whole drive had been spent pursued by images of decay, destruction of this olive forest looked on without end. In that luxuriant prospect, in that monotonous enormous growing, there was death's clearest proclamation, more certain than is found in any ruin.

The Arctic Ocean

Eight-thirty in the morning Tokyo time, July the twenty-first; while London time is eight P.M., the evening of the previous day. The aeroplane flies over the arctic regions. For a long time a sea of cloud, like cast off fragments of thick wool, had buried all the under sky; and at the edge of that a red sun floated, one did not know whether of dawn or sunset.

Then a rent suddenly opened in the cloud, and the sea showed itself. Layer after layer of cloud, so only when the gaps in all came cleverly together could one see, terrifyingly far-off below, a tiny fragment of the ocean.

Looking at that sea I was a boy again, remembering a winter morning of my distant childhood. The sheet of ice inside my bucket starts to melt, and that small vessel is filled with a weird color, mixture of white and blue and black.

Something as cold, something as stark as that, is what there must be in the nether world, there in the lowest depths of hell.

Dawning

When I open the top of a new ink bottle there are sea depths of blue and black. How small the Indian and Pacific oceans when compared to this. Like a brain surgeon I put on pure white, wash my hands in disinfectant; and then get down to work, cutting away portions of these depths, collecting them in this small cylindrical instrument.

New currents start to flow within the ocean. Great herds of whales, attended by countless predatory ravens and schools of flying fish, have made their way through S. canal and now are swarming into the deep gulfs of K.

The tide begins to roar; a whirlpool forms. A warship, of unknown nationality, slides over a sea whose surface keeps on falling.

It seems that it will soon be day.

The River Indus

That in the Indus basin one should find a huge ruined city; that countless fragments should be dug up there, remnants of what must have been high civilization, one of refinement, purity, and splendor; and that this civilization should have vanished from the earth, in one night at the onset of a flood; well, there is nothing much to be surprised at in all that.

However, this has one truly horrifying aspect. Under this city they again dug up another one exactly like it. Out from under the marketplace came yet another marketplace, under each storehouse similar storehouses; and roads appeared from under roads, drinking fountains under drinking fountains. The ancient Indus peoples built their capital on the buried one, a perfect replica set on the top of it, like one thin biscuit placed upon another.

Horror at this was not felt just by me. That moment the dual city was discovered, "decadence" took on its proper meaning, became alive and new to us again as though it never had been used before. We understood how the whole human race, beginning from these ancient Indus peoples, had been traveling one straight road of decadence. The sentence of our final dissolution, our vanishing from the surface of the earth, was then made over us, immediately, allowing no extenuating pleas.

The upper reaches of the Indus are a turbid yellow. In its mid course it shows a rust-like redness. Then at its lowest reaches it achieves the pale thin color of a fish, and so flows out into the sea.

The Boy

The boy got off the train at a town in the north, well known for its great fires in the quick hot weather. It was the season when large pomegranates are lined up on greengrocer's stalls. The boy stayed there for two days, hoping to see the sky burn red with flame; but nothing happened.

The boy took the night train farther north; moved to a town where mirages occurred. The town was thronged with people for the festival; the sea glimpsed at the end of streets was rough. The boy stayed there for two days more; small driftwood floating on a sea where nothing strange seemed likely to occur.

Three days later the boy got down at an unknown station on the peninsular. He walked the narrow, walled, fish-smelling streets; came out upon a cliff. The sea was spread before him; the sunset sky of a breathtaking beauty. And so he threw himself down from the cliff there. He did not know it, but in that region this spot was famous for the number of its suicides.

River Light

The stone steps went steep down to the water's surface. At high tide they were covered halfway up, but when the tide was out the lowest cleared the water, covered with seaweed and small shells.

When I was there washing my hands one early evening, the soap suddenly slipped from me. As if alive it tailed and flipped in the water, and then was gone, sunken in those depths. Later I felt an enormous sense of loss, because no matter what I did it would not come back twice into my hands.

This happened when I was a boy, and since then I have never had a loss quite so complete as that. For I had understood that river light, that light still held in water when the rest is dark, is different from all other forms of light; a light preceding tragedy's last curtain.

The Beginning of Autumn

That morning, as I quit my bed, something like a bird's shadow crossed my mind, flashed over me for a moment, then was gone. I do not know if it was light or dark; I do not know if it was warm or cold. That day, all day, I thought only of something like a bird's shadow.

That evening, as I took my walk, I found a tiny puddle hidden in thick grass. As I gazed down at it I faintly heard the dripping sound of water. I tried to listen closely, but I did not hear the sound again.

That night I slept among things like bird shadows, like sounds of dripping water. I spent the night enclosed in these uncertainties. And so I could find rest, protected as I slept by vague, uncertain things.

The Kite

    One by one the children raised their kites in the field. Fanned by a fierce wind all swung and wound as they rose. Only my kite would not go up. I jerked on the string, but headlong down again it crashed, striking into the frost, piercing the black earth of the fields.

    Far-off days of my youth, flashes of white winter sunlight scattered by the wind, now I think of you. And now I know it was no kite I raised, but solitude; and no, not solitude, but death. I raised up death into that fierce wind. And then I ran among the stubble of the fields; picked up that death which cruelly fell and struck.

Green Leaves

In an age when there were still gods in the world, one loyal warrior stopped his horse in a tree's shade, entrusting to his son the task that still remained. And so they parted. I do not know who wrote the tale, but the image of the shade's gray dark through which a fresh breeze blows, that pleases me. No mournful drama now of parting in green leaves, but only this pleasantness of shade remains, brief interval well made.

The gods have vanished from the world now, but still that space in time is here. I set the things of those I love, the kennel of my dog, the small desk of my innocent granddaughter, under the shade of the tree. My happiness, too, is not remote from thoughts of parting.

Youth

With one sheet of poems in my pocket, I visited a poet in the country who taught school there. Dinner over, when I took my leave, outside a snowstorm blew. I wrapped my cloak about my head, hurrying for the station down closed streets where all was shuttered tight. In the waiting room I sat close to the stove, along with a girl in a scarf who was there already. The name of the station was Stone's Throw.

In the forty years since then how many times have I recalled that scene; each time the image going further off and small. The town of Stone's Throw in the falling snow then appears as a row of closed sea shells. The station too is one of those sea shells. My twenty-year-old life enclosed in a seashell.

Darkly, mournfully, some pure absolute appears, brushing aside the snow. Smothered in snow it waits as things approach; waits for the shining fields of flowers; waits for the busy marketplaces; waits for the audience chambers with their brilliant chandeliers.

Minute by minute waiting their approach.

One Month, One Day

I throw aside my book and go downtown. The town is now half buried in the sand, no sign of any life remaining. I enter an empty bar and wait for twilight. This office block is all laid waste; I go on the roof and wait for the moon to rise.

Twilight does not come, and no moon rises. Night falls like the fall of rain. I walk from one street to another. Following the logic of the bat's wing-beat I walk, turning at sharp right angles. At the first turning I meet with my dead father. At the fourth turning I pass by my living son. From that point on I hear a strange-toned music. The sea surrounds this town; it is the sound of the sea as its surface falls.

Elegy

Five days after you died a wind blew and brought down the last leaves on the oak. One month after you died there was a small earthquake. And thirty-nine days after you died it snowed. On the night of that next day snow fell again. And then all day the next day after that, a peaceful winter sun shone down, bringing a rare red sunset in the evening. The trees were black beyond remaining patches of white snow, and the red sky combed all those trees together, scattering flecks of fire about them. I sat on a chair on the porch and watched it; and then for the very first time I could believe that you were now no longer in the world. And then I heard it for the first time too; in that funereal, mourning landscape, the sound of a bell which kept on tolling for you.

The Pool

Now I want a passionate summer like that far-off day. Perhaps that day was all the summer I have ever had. The path along the cliff is smothered deep in grass, and I am running there. Red flowers like blood bloom down the river side, and up in the hills the cicada sing like rain. And I was running in a place like that. Burned in the violent sun of early afternoon, all that was living was myself, and the grasshoppers scattering before me. The villagers, the villagers were dead, all in their separate houses, all fallen in the attitudes they'd chosen. So I was hurrying by the river to that pool, shaped like an inkwell among rocks and ferns, running to hurl myself within it.

The Ancient Capital

Flocks of pigeons fill the ancient mosque. The tower is blue; blue which has had the soul sucked out of it. A bazaar is open to the left of this; camels, donkeys, men, all put in the same mixer. Everything here is of historical interest, but the ruins of the ancient citadel (to the right hand of the mosque) preserve their former shape the best; an area of sand enclosed by castle walls (the crenellation has all been worn away) in which a town of say one hundred thousand souls could easily be absorbed. Just a huge amphitheater in the desert. Whenever you look small troops of camel pass; but yet they only pass, for here there grows not one tree, nor one blade of grass. Which is all no doubt just how it should be, for this is the capital of the ancient Bactrian peoples.

At midday if you strain your ears you hear perhaps the cries of ghosts two thousand years of age. It may be also that eighth-century ghosts, those slaughtered by the Arabs, and of those too, massacred by Mongols in the thirteenth, respectfully keep silent here while listening to those cries. There are so many elders who preceded them.

Old Man in a Turban

He sat on the expanse of grass, crosslegged in contemplation, an old man in a turban. When he opened his eyes I asked him what he prayed for. He said he prayed for freedom from all mind, all thought. I asked him then how one might enter these mindless regions. He said you hold the tongue in the center of the mouth, making quite sure its sides touch against nothing.

In foreign countries, in hotels at dawn, I have at times tried squatting on my bed, straight-backed, doing the way he said. And then sometimes the flames flicker about me; or a bleak north wind is blowing through the room; or a winter shower falls and passes by. I am the guardian deity, god of fire; I am the great Zen poet on Cold Mountain; I am the Foundling, his companion.*

Opening my eyes I feel myself in exile. I get down from the bed and open the window. The desert I have traveled for over a month now, sleeps in the dark before dawn. The bazaar which must, once again today, barter off all its last remaining jewels, is sleeping too. Then I recall the old man in the turban, seeing the face of a man who is alone. The face of a man in exile for scores of years now.

---

* See Introduction p. 54; also Burton Watson, trans., *Cold Mountain*, Columbia University Press, New York, 1970, p. 7.

The Evening Sun

On the day the long rains ended I sat on the veranda of my study, spent half the day there looking over the garden covered in rank grass. I understood my past was like that too, days all covered over in rank grass. I looked back down that one long road, covered in rank grass, and tried to gather up the days when things went wrong. But I could not work out the days when things went wrong. I tried to find the days when things went right; but nor could I work out the days when things went right. All were buried deep down in thick grass. All that remained in memory was this: walking toward a burning evening sun.

When, in what day or year, I do not know. But I am walking passionately toward one portion of the inflamed and burning heavens.

Soaked in the burning sky's scatter of flame, I and the grasses burying the world about me, we all burn fiercely red.

A Light Rain in Autumn

"I want to become much, much smaller so no one can find me," my infant granddaughter said. Then she crouched down again behind the tree stump, with eager face making herself as small as she could. She was playing hide and seek.

"I want to become much, much smaller so no one can find me." Those were good words, I thought, walking all day over dead leaves in the garden. At evening, as it might have been expected, a light fall of rain began.

"I want to become much, much smaller so no one can find me." I drew my body in, the way my granddaughter had, facing the empty sheet of writing paper. From midnight on the sound of the rain grew heavy.

Travel

At the beginning of each year I make my travel plans.

For 1967, Peshawar.

The Summer Palace of the Kushan kings.

A town of many pomegranate trees.

The castle town where Alexander took his after-dinner sleep.

In the room of my hotel among the hills, I shall pen a letter to my other self in Tokyo, written in unintelligible, spidery script, finally breaking off relations with him.

BIOGRAPHIES

MIYOSHI TATSUJI

Miyoshi Tatsuji was born in Osaka on August 23, 1900, the eldest son of ten children, five of whom died in infancy. His father was a printer, and the family were not well off. While still a baby he was "adopted" by a family in Maizuru (on the Japan Sea coast), but since he was the eldest son this adoption was illegal, and he was soon taken in by his grandparents, who lived in the country in Hyōgo Prefecture. He attended primary school there, but a nervous breakdown at the age of eight (he had nightmares about death every night) resulted in his being sent back home to Osaka. This homecoming did not last long, however, and he returned once more to his grandparents, this time together with his elder sister. It is not surprising that his first book of poems should show so much concern about his mother.

In 1913 he returned home for good, and entered school in Osaka. His academic record was slightly below average, but he started reading the leading novelists of the time, Natsume Sōseki and Tokutomi Rōka (or Kenjirō), and also became absorbed in the paintings of Takehisa Yumeji.

On graduating in 1913, he helped at home with the family business for a year, then entered junior high school where he started to write *haiku* under the influence of the *Hototogisu* (the new, realist) school. He is said to have written well over one thousand during his teens. However, for financial reasons, he left this school in the September of the following year, 1915, and entered the Junior Army Cadet School in compliance with his father's wishes. This was a rare step for a boy of his social class at that time. In 1918 he went on to the Central Cadet School in Tokyo, spending a year and a half there before being posted to Northern Korea as an officer cadet. In 1920 he entered the Military Academy, but left in 1921 for reasons which have never been made clear. He went back to

169

Osaka to try to run the shaky family business more efficiently, but he got on so badly with his father that at one time he thought of emigrating to Mexico, and began learning Spanish. This idea was eventually given up under family pressure. During this period his main literary interest was in the *waka* of Yosano Akiko and Kitahara Hakushū. This same year the family business failed, and the father disappeared from home, never to return.

In April of 1922 he entered high school in Kyoto, where he met, among others, the poet Maruyama Kaoru. His interests now began to move toward the poem, in particular the poems of Hagiwara Sakutarō and the translations from the French of Horiguchi Daigaku, although he still wrote almost none himself. In 1925 he entered the French department of Tokyo University (he had learned French while an army cadet). He was now reading the Japanese symbolist poets, and is said to have memorized hundreds of their poems. He was particularly attracted by Satō Haruo and Kitahara Hakushū, but the perfection of their work made him despair of writing poems of his own. However, he was writing, and also making literary friendships: first with the short-story writer Kajii Motojirō (whose work influenced Miyoshi's prose poems to some extent), then with Kitagawa Fuyuhiko and Kawabata Yasunari. By 1927 his poems were being published, and it was in this year that he first met Hagiwara Sakutarō. The relationship of master and pupil was established between them, and remained unaltered throughout the remainder of both their lives.

On graduating from Tokyo University in 1928 he was due to enter a publishing house, but since it went bankrupt he turned to translating as a way of earning a living, producing one hundred thousand pages of translations over the next ten years (that figure should be divided by three to gain some sense, in English terms, of the labor involved). He completed his translation of Baudelaire's *The Spleen of Paris* in 1928, and it was published the next year. These have become a translation classic, although the main factor of interest about them in this context is how little concern he shows with musical, rhythmical values. This same tendency can be seen in much translation into Japanese of French poetry during this period, if one contrasts it with the forms such translated poetry had previously taken. He was now writing prolifically, both translations and original work, and 1930 saw the publication of his first book of poems, *The Survey Ship*, which was well received. His next, in 1932, was written in the lyrical quatrains which were to dominate his poetry for the next few years, and and in 1933 he also published *tanka*.

In 1934 he married the niece of Satō Haruo (his previous engagement to Hagiwara's beautiful sister, Ai, had been broken off, although he did eventually marry her for a short period in 1944). His first volume of *waka* appeared in that year, as also did the magazine *Shiki* (*The Seasons*), with which Miyoshi was closely associated. The lyrical tradition this magazine represented was to dominate Japanese poetry for a decade or so.

Little more need be recorded here, except that he was now a central figure in the Japanese poetic scene, remaining so until the re-emergence of modernism after the war, by which time his reputation was such that no alterations in fashion could affect him. The volume of poems he published in 1939, *Haru no misaki* (*Spring headland*, a bringing together of his first four books), is said to have sold over 200,000 copies, an unprecedented number for any modern Japanese poet. This indicates how readers have seen even his first book as in the lyrical rather than the modernist tradition.

The postwar years saw a more bitter, even desperate tone in his poetry, as his interests moved toward the Chinese poets. He died in 1964, his fine critical work on his master, Hagiwara, having appeared in the previous year.

ANZAI FUYUE
(Not to be confused with Anzai Hitoshi [1919–])

Anzai Fuyue was born in Nara on March 9, 1898, into a samurai family. His father was chief secretary in the Prefectural Governor's Office, but transferred to the Ministry of Education in Tokyo in the following year. Anzai's teens were spent in Sakai, near Osaka, where his father was now headmaster of a school, reading a great deal of Chinese literature (his father's interest). At school he was a noted athlete in swimming and rowing.

In 1920 his mother died, and he accompanied his father, who had taken up a post as manager of a trading company, to Port Arthur in Manchuria. In 1927 Anzai began working for Manchurian Railways, but the severe cold led to arthritis of his right knee, and the operation resulted in the loss of that leg. Blood transfusions kept him alive, and he was able to leave the hospital after a year and a half of convalescence.

During this period of recovery he wrote and in 1924, with Kitagawa, whom he had met in the previous year, and two others, he formed the magazine *A* (this character is used to write "Asia," and presumably means that here). In 1928 *A* ceased publication, and Anzai joined the magazine *Poetry and Poetics*. In this year he also married, and was becoming known as a writer. A son was born in 1929, the year of publication of *The Warship Mari*. Two more books of poems came out in 1933, but neither has the interest of his first, and the modernist movement was now virtually at an end. In 1934, on the death of his father, he returned to Sakai. He was employed in the municipal office there, mostly in the editing of official publications, a post in which he remained until 1952. A fourth book of poems appeared in 1943, and in the postwar period he was active in various fields of the arts in Osaka, particularly in radio and television, creating *avante-garde* pieces of electronic music. He was also active as a member of committees on education, broadcasting, etc. Among his considerable number of unpublished works were more than a hundred songs for school and other civic purposes.

Anzai is a case of someone flowering briefly as a poet, and then devoting himself to a useful and honorable life connected with the arts and education in the provinces. Although he was associated with a number of poetry magazines in the early 1930s and during the modernist revival of the postwar period, the poetry he wrote showed, as Kitagawa Fuyuhiko has said, a growing (and growingly incommunicable) self-obsession. Something of this can be seen in his first book as well, although in that case the strong personal energy behind the writing seems to give poetic life to it. It would, however, be easy to bring the charge of dilettantism against his later work, and difficult to refute.

He entered the hospital in 1965 with what was thought to be a mild skin inflammation, but died nineteen days later, a very quiet and beautiful death according to those who witnessed it. The unexpected, seemingly accidental nature of his end is very much of a piece with the making of him as a poet, and also with the tone of the poems which were then made.

TAMURA RYŪICHI

Tamura Ryūichi was born in Ōtsuka, Tokyo, on March 18, 1923, the year of the Great Kanto Earthquake. He was the eldest son of a restaurant proprietor, a leading figure in the neighborhood since he was one of the founder members of the union of local restaurants, geisha houses, and houses of assignation. Tamura was consistently and seriously ill for the first ten years of his life, but playing baseball at school (where all the children belonged to the same, outdated *"demi-monde"* as himself) strengthened him. His entrance into junior high school in 1935 gave him his first experience of release from that world, but he found the commercial subjects he was obliged to study incomprehensible and boring. In his fourth year, at the invitation of a classmate, the poet Kitamura Tarō, he became a "member" of the little magazines *Le Bal* and *Shinryōdo* (*New Territory*). He thus came to know middle-class poets such as Ayukawa Nobuo, who were university students at that time, and their conversation created a quite different world from the one he had grown up in. He was mainly affected by the European literature of the 1920s, for he found traditional Japanese poetry, as well as that of Hagiwara Sakutarō and Takamura Kōtarō, of no interest. His own commitment to the writing of poetry was still only slight (although he did write some), for "poetry" was principally something which existed as a way out of the anachronistic world of his childhood. His experience of the war years extended this feeling of antipathy beyond the concept of Ōtsuka to that of Japan in general.

In March of 1940 he graduated from school, but turned down the job which had been found for him in the Tokyo Gas Company, and decided to go on to the university. Since he had no intention of studying for any examination (his principal motive was military deferment) he aimed at the private universities whose examination requirements were mere formalities at that time, spending the time reading (an average of two books a day) and lounging about with his poet friends. He entered Meiji University in 1941. As his older friends began to be drafted he found he could no longer write poems, and his intellectual interests began to move away from the French moralists to Japanese ones, then to the traditional *rakugo* (comic story-telling) and the local entertainment halls. In December 1943, an emergency call-up saw him in the navy, but when the war ended he had still not seen action but was enjoying swimming every day in the Japan Sea during the beautiful weather of that August.

On returning to Tokyo he found that Ōtsuka had vanished from the surface of the earth, and the past with it.

In 1947 the magazine *Arechi* (*The Waste Land*), of which he edited the first three numbers, appeared, leading to the formation of The Waste Land Group of poets. This group produced an annual anthology from 1951 to 1958, and dominated the poetic scene of this period. His first book of poems, *Four Thousand Days and Nights*, was published in 1956, and a second, *Kotoba no nai Sekai* (*World Without Language*) in 1962, the result of three years spent in the mountains. Much of the passionate lyricism of the first volume is absent in this second one, which shows a colder, more objective concern with language and the poetic constructs made out of it. Opinion in Japan remains divided upon the new direction Tamura's poetry took at this point, but many of the younger critics have tended to disapprove. A *Collected Poems* appeared in 1966, and this has been followed by *Midori no Shisō* (*A Green Thought*), 1967, and *Shinnen no Tegami* (*New Year's Letter*) in 1973. He remains, with Yoshioka Minoru, the most distinguished of Japanese postwar poets.

YOSHIOKA MINORU

Yoshioka Minoru was born in Tokyo on April 15, 1919, into a working-class family. He dreamed of being a sculptor after leaving school in 1934 (a desire which has had an influence upon his poetry), but went to work for a publisher of medical books, attending trade school in the evenings. At the age of sixteen he was reading the novels of Shiga Naoya and Akutagawa Ryūnosuke, then the poetry of Yosano Buson, Satō Haruo, and Kitahara Hakushū. He feels that this last writer has had a considerable influence upon him. He began by writing *haiku* and *waka*, but turned to poems at the age of nineteen, as a result of reading Kitazone Katsue (the modernist poet who is mentioned in the writings of Ezra Pound), and also the poems of Picasso. He says that he was trying to imitate these writers, although he still admired the different kind of poetry of Miyoshi Tatsuji, whom he was reading at the same time. Of the other poetry he read after this he considers that of Takamura Kōtarō, Hagiwara Sakutarō, Saitō Mokichi (a writer in the traditional forms), Nishiwaki Junzaburō, and the *Arechi* anthologies as relevant to his own work.

Writing was interrupted for five years by the war. He was enlisted in 1940, but saw no action since he was employed in looking after horses. In 1940 he brought out a slim, privately printed volume (100 copies), *Konsui Kisetsu (Trance Season)*, but his next book, *Seibutsu (Still Life)*, was not to appear for another fifteen years. Clearly the war destroyed the past as much for Yoshioka as it did for Tamura, although in Yoshioka's case it produced more of a tragic realization, as if he himself had died along with it. By the time the war ended both his parents were dead.

Seibutsu in 1955 was also privately printed, and was followed in 1958 by *Sōryo (The Priests)*, which was awarded the H prize (the equivalent for poets of the Akutagawa prize for novelists). He married in 1959, and in that year brought out a volume of his early *waka* (70 copies), a ritual gesture of farewell to the past they represented. His *Collected Poems* appeared in 1967.

Yoshioka works for the large publishing house of Chikuma Shobō, and is known as a book designer. His tastes and style of living, as is clear from the interviews he has given, are very much those of the ordinary Japanese businessman, which makes the existence of these remarkable poems even more extraordinary. One of these interviews can be found in Hiroaki Sato, ed., *Anthology of Modern Japanese Poets, Chicago Review* 25, No. 2, 1973. His most recent book of poetry, *Safuran Tsumi (Gathering Saffron)* in 1976, won him the Takami Jun prize for that year, and is probably the finest volume of poetry to have appeared in Japanese in the 1970s.

Yoshioka has said that he is a "*haiku*-like" person, although he dislikes the "wetness" (sentimentality) which sometimes goes with traditional writing. He sees *The Priests* as written against such "wetness." He believes that his poems are written for special people, principally, in fact, for himself, yet still feels that they are more traditional than *avante-garde*, since art requires a form which can be given to it only by tradition. Many critics share this view that his poetry is not truly modernist, maintaining that his war experiences have given him so powerful a neurosis that the form in which it works itself out goes against modernist poetic theory. Much of the writing on his poems, indeed, treats them as objects for pathological analysis (the entry in *Nihon Kindai Bungaku Jiten*, 1977, iii, 470, for example), which seems to imply they have not truly become poems. Such statements assume that modernism demands a complete coldness of the creator before his artifact, which may well be true in theory but which very few poets ever attain even if they wish to do so. However, if a concern with clear images which do not relate to each other in any logical or prose-like way is accepted as one of the central aspects of modernism, then his poetry has remained as much within that tradition as the early prose poems of his given here.

TANIKAWA SHUNTARŌ

Tanikawa Shuntarō was born in Tokyo on December 15, 1931, the only child of the philosopher Tanikawa Tetsuzō. He claims to have come into being through the desire of his grandfather for a grandson, for his parents themselves had not wished for a child. At primary school he did well, although he did not enjoy it, and this dislike also persisted through to junior high school. However, listening to Beethoven was a revelation indicating that life was possible (this experience took place during the immediate postwar period), and that life must be realized through language, although not only the language of poetry. His use of so many literary forms can be traced back to this revelation.

At the age of eighteen he began writing poetry, and by this time his loathing of school had grown so great, and his grades had fallen so low, that it was decided that he should not go on to the university. In December of this same year, 1949, five of his poems appeared in the magazine *Bungakkai* (*World of Literature*), as a result of the influence of Miyoshi Tatsuji, who was a friend of the family and had a high opinion of Tanikawa's talent. He was quickly recognized as one of the leading lights of the postwar poetic scene, a position confirmed by his first book in 1952. This work, *Nijū Oku Kōnen no Kodoku* (*Two Billion Light Years of Solitude*), treats life on a cosmic scale over an enormous time span, as the title indicates. The desire to continue expanding the subject matter of poetry ("To know everything, to have all my questions answered," as he puts it in his earliest published poem) is a constant note throughout his career.

Marriage in 1954 ended in divorce a year later. He married again in 1957. His writings of the 1950's reflect this in their reliance upon the sensibilities (rather than being the ideological constructs aimed at by prewar modernism)—an aspect they share with most modernist poetry of the same period, as one can see in the case of Tamura and, to some extent, of Yoshioka. In the 1960s, however, a more satirical note began to take over. He also turned to other artistic forms, such as the drama, the film of the Tokyo Olympics, design of pavilions for the Osaka World Exposition, children's songs, and books combining poems with paintings or photographs. *Collected Poems* appeared in 1965.

In the 1970s a number of children's books (including a five-volume translation of *Mother Goose*, which attempt to exploit verbal playfulness in Japanese in the way it has been done in English, a collection of essays, six very fine film scenarios, as well as the book of prose poems given here, indicate the ever-expanding nature of his interests.

INOUE YASUSHI

Inoue Yasushi was born in Hokkaido on May 6th, 1907, the eldest son of an army doctor. The Inoues have a history as doctors going back to the eighteenth century. His father was constantly being posted to various parts of the country, so in 1913 he was sent to the family home in Yugashima on the Izu peninsula. Here he was brought up by his "grandmother" who was, in fact, only the former mistress of his grandfather. The old woman and boy spent six years together in a storehouse separated from the main building and its inhabitants, since she was an object of contempt and animosity for the other members of the family, and for the people of the village. The images of solitude and endurance one finds in his literature mostly have their origins in the fierce sense of unity he felt with her. She appears in his novels quite often.

On her death in 1920 he returned to his parents, but in 1922 his father was posted to Taiwan and Inoue was sent to Mishima (to a house connected with his dead "grandmother") and went to school there. He did not study very hard there or in high school in Kanazawa in 1927, when he was obsessed with judo. On graduating he gave up the idea of being a doctor, and returned to the literary interests of his junior high school days, submitting poems to a magazine called *Nihon Kai Shijin* (*Japan Sea Poets*), edited by the rural poet mentioned in the poem "Youth."

In 1930 he entered the law school of Kyushu University, but found the lectures of no interest and went to Tokyo and took lodgings there. Here he became a "member" of a magazine run by a former *Minshūha* poet, Fukuda Masao, meeting a number of anarchist and dadaist writers, as the son of the house he was lodging at was an anarchist himself. This was the period during which Marxism was gradually being driven underground, and political concern among the young was at a height. However, Inoue himself always remained an indifferent watcher of events (see the poem, "The Eye"). After two years of official attendance at Kyushu University he entered the philosophy department of Kyoto University, and lived in Kyoto. Although he still managed to avoid attending classes, his student life finally came to an end with his graduation in 1936.

During this period in Kyoto he had written novels, plays, and film scenarios, and won prize money for them, finding that he could always make money by writing, although the writing itself gave him little satisfaction. In 1935 he married the daughter of a professor of Kyoto University who was also a relative, a nephew of Inoue's grandfather brought up within the Inoue household. This was a deliberate attempt to make him settle down, which seems to have been successful, for Inoue entered the editorial department of the *Sunday Mainichi* newspaper in Osaka in 1936. He found the job there to his taste and dropped the idea of being a novelist. His new life was then disturbed by his enlistment in 1937 (with the outbreak of war with China); he was sent to Northern China, where he became ill and was discharged in April of the next year. This is something not related in his literature (except in the poem, "The Eye," where it is only mentioned), but it seems to have had a decisive effect upon him as a person.

The ending of the Pacific War gave him a new lease on creative life. He wrote a considerable number of poems, and the years 1947 and 1948 saw the publication of two novellas, *Tōgyū* (*The Bull Fight*) and *Ryōjū* (*The Shotgun* or *The Hunting Gun*, twice translated into English under those respective titles), which gained him the Akutagawa prize and established him as a leading novelist.

In 1951 he left the newspaper to devote himself to writing. His novels are of the "middlebrow" kind, although superior examples of the genre. Perhaps the most interesting are the historical ones, for Inoue's interest in history is deep, as one can see in his prose poems, which of all his writings should live the longest.

ORIGINAL TITLES OF THE TRANSLATED POEMS

MIYOSHI TATSUJI
from *Sokuryōsen* ('The Survey Ship'), 1930.

Kodama, Mura, Haru, Mura, Tōge, Machi, Niwa, Niwa, Hiru, *Memoire, Enfance Finie*, Kiji, Kozue no hanashi. (Note: the last poem is from *Sokuryōsen Shūi* (i.e., "additional poems").

ANZAI FUYUE
from *Gunkan Mari* ("The Warship Mari"), 1929.

Mifuyu no sho, Niwa, Tanjōbi, Futatabi tanjōbi, *Call*, Himawari wa mō kuroi tamakusuri, Saikoro, Marunu no kinenbi, Kakō, Tsugumi, Ichijiku, Michi.

TAMURA RYŪICHI
from *Yonsen no hi to yoru* ("Four Thousand Days and Nights"), 1956.

Fukokuga, Shizumeru tera, Ōgon gensō, Aki, Koe, Yokan, Imeji, Kōtei, Fuyu no ongaku.

YOSHIOKA MINORU
from *Sōryo* ("The Priests"), 1958.

Kigeki, Kokuhaku, Shima, Densetsu, Fuyu no e, Tanjun, Kokei, Kaifuku, Utsukushii tabi.

TANIKAWA SHUNTARŌ
from *Teigi* ("Definitions"), 1975.

Nandemonai mono no songen, Hasami, Koppu no fukanō no sekkin, Koppu o miru kutsū to kairaku ni tsuite, Ringo e no koshitsu, Seisoku no jōken, Hai ni tsuite no shiken, Mizuasobi no kansatsu, Yo no owari no tame no saibu, Gijikaibōgakuteki na jigazō, Hikareta mado no aru bunrei.

INOUE YASUSHI

from *Hokkoku* ('The North Country'), 1958.

Kōgen, Kamaitachi, Shōgai, Hitomi, Aijō, Aru tabitachi, Rokugatsu.

from *Chichūkai* ('The Mediterranean'), 1962.

Oriibu no hayashi, Hokkyokuken no umi, Akegata, Indasu gawa, Shōnen.

from *Unga* ('The Canal'), 1967.

Kawa akari, Aki no hajime.

from *Kisetsu* ('Seasons'), 1971.

Tako, Aoba, Seishun, Bōgetsu bōjitsu, Banka, Fuchi.

from *Enseiro* ('The Expeditionary Route'), 1976.

Koto Barufu, Tāban no rōjin, Yūbae, Shigure, Tabi.

Index

A, 46, 172
Akutagawa Ryūnosuke, 175
alexandrine, 4, 50
Anzai Fuyue, 14, 44, 46-48, 79-93, 172-173
Anzai Hitoshi, 172
Arechi, see *Waste Land, The*
Ayukawa Nobuo, 174

Bal, Le, 174
Bashō, see Matsuo Bashō
Baudelaire, Charles, v, 3, 12, 15-25, 27, 33, 41, 43, 44, 52, 170
Bertrand, Aloysius, 15, 20, 25
blank verse, 4, 19, 50

Cameron, Norman, 52

Democratic School, The (*Minshūha*), 12, 41, 45, 46, 179

five-seven rhythm, 8, 11, 50
Flaubert, Gustave, 12, 36
'free poem' (*vers libre*), 12, 41, 45, 48
fu, 3
Fukuda Masao, 179

Guys, Constantin, 25

Hagiwara Ai, 171
Hagiwara Sakutarō, 7, 11-13, 41-44, 170, 171, 174, 176
haibun, 45
haiku, 7, 11, 45, 46, 169, 175, 176
heroic couplet, 5
Horiguchi Daigaku, 170

Inoue Yasushi, 51, 54, 141-166, 179-181

ka (or *uta*), 7, 8
Kaichō-on, see *Sound of the Tide, The*
Kajii Motojirō, 170
Kambara Ariake, 10, 13
Kawabata Yasunari, 170
Kitagawa Fuyuhiko, 14, 47, 173
Kitahara Hakushū, 10, 13, 170, 175
Kitamura Tarō, 174
Kitazono Katsue, 175

Mallarmé, Stéphane, 12, 32-40
Manyōshū, 8
Maruyama Kaoru, 170
Matsuo Bashō, 3, 47
Medieval Latin Lyric, 9
Minshūha, see Democratic School, The
Miyoshi Tatsuji, 7, 13, 14, 44-46, 48, 52-53, 59-77, 169-171, 176, 178

Natsume Sōseki, 169
New Prose Poem Movement, v, 14, 44, 46
New Territory (Shinryōdo), 174
Nishiwaki, Junzaburō, 11-12, 176

Oak Tree (Shii no ki), 45
Ōoka Makoto, 50
Ossian, 5

Picasso, Pablo, 176
Poetry and Poetics (Shi to Shiron), 13, 14
Pound, Ezra, 175
Proletarian literary movement, 12

185

Rimbaud, Arthur, 4, 12, 15, 25-32, 37

Saitō Mokichi, 176
Sartre, Jean-Paul, 123
Satō Haruo, 170, 171, 175
Seasons, The, 171
Sei Shōnagon, 3
Selection of New Style Poems (Shintaishishō), 10, 12
shi, 7, 8
Shi to Shiron, see *Poetry and Poetics*
Shiga Naoya, 175
Shii no ki, see *Oak Tree*
Shiki, see *Seasons, The*
Shimazaki Tōson, 10
Shinryōdo, see *New Territory*
Shintaishishō, see *Selection of New Style Poems*
Short Poem Movement, 46
Sound of the Tide, The (Kaichō-on), 10
Symbolist movement in Japanese poetry, 10

Takamura Kōtarō, 174, 175

Takehisa Yumeji, 169
Tamura Ryūichi, vi, 14, 48-49, 95-106, 173-175, 178
Tanikawa Shuntarō, 49, 51, 53, 125-140, 177-179
Tanikawa Tetsuzō, 177
Tokutomi Rōka, 169

Ueda Bin, 10
uta, see *ka*

Valéry, Paul, 3
Verlaine, Paul, 45
verse libre, see 'free poem'
Virgil, 8

waka, 7, 11, 171, 175
Waste Land, The (Arechi), 175, 176
Watson, Burton, 163(n.)

Yosano Akiko, 170
Yosano Buson, 175
Yoshioka Minoru, vi, 14, 48-49, 107-123, 175-177, 178
Young, Edward, 5

LIBRARY OF CONGRESS CATALOGING IN PUBLICATION DATA

Main entry under title:

The Modern Japanese prose poem.

1. Prose poems, Japanese—Translations into English.
2. Prose poems, English—Translations from Japanese.
I. Keene, Dennis, 1934-
PL782.E3M65   895.6'1'4508   79-16809
ISBN 0-691-06418-0

GPSR Authorized Representative: Easy Access System Europe - Mustamäe tee
50, 10621 Tallinn, Estonia, gpsr.requests@easproject.com

www.ingramcontent.com/pod-product-compliance
Lightning Source LLC
Chambersburg PA
CBHW051524230426
43668CB00012B/1737